Note to Parents

CONTENT

Section 1: 32 Representatives
You will meet the representative from each group of basic Chinese Alphabets.

Section 2: Basic Alphabets
All the basic Chinese Alphabets are grouped into 32 teams according to their appearance and stroke patterns.

Section 3: 32 Teams of Basic Alphabets
Basic Chinese Alphabets are repeated in this section in smaller font and shown in teams for easy comparison within each team.

Section 4: Variations and Exceptions
Variations of basic Chinese Alphabets are created by making a slight change, e.g. change or add a stroke. **Exceptions** are alphabets with different stroke patterns from the basic alphabets.

WHY LEARN CHINESE ALPHABETS

More Efficient and Effective Way to Learn
If thousands of Chinese characters are learnt by combining single strokes, you will need to put in more effort to remember and distinguish them.

This new way of learning is by combining common parts (alphabets and strokes) into characters, something like forming English words (but not exactly the same).

What-You-See-Is-What-You-Name
The Alphabets are named according to their appearance to help you remember them. For example, some are named according to English letters 'C', 'n' and 'L'.

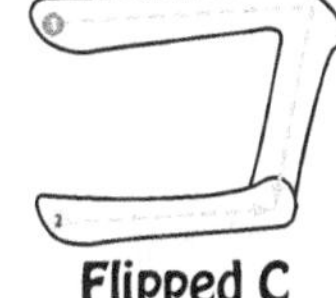
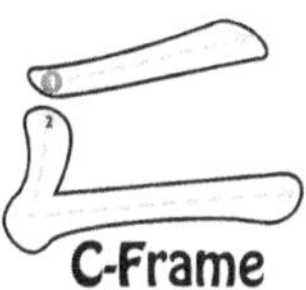

Flipped C   C-Frame

WHAT YOUR CHILD WILL LEARN

A) 32 Representative Chinese Alphabets
In the first section, go through all the 32 Chinese Alphabets representing each group. Read out their names and observe how they describe the alphabet. For example,

Parallels

B) 32 Teams of Chinese Alphabets
This alphabet will appear again in Sections 2 and 3 with other alphabets sharing similar stroke patterns. For instance, alphabets with (almost) parallel strokes are in the same team. Each team has 3 to 6 basic alphabets.

Parallels

C) Variations and Exceptions
Variations of some basic Chinese Alphabets are introduced in the last section.
Exceptions are alphabets that have different stroke order from the basic alphabets.

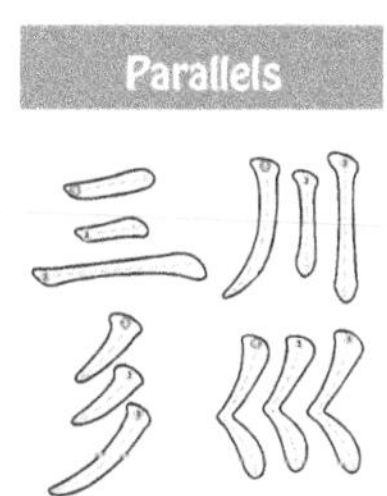

Basic

Variation

这 是

This book
belongs to

的 书。

What I can do in this book

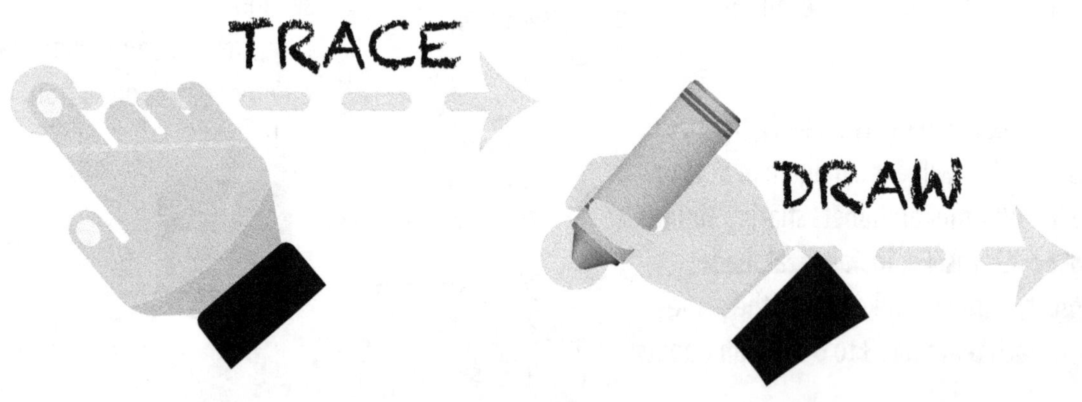

CHINESE ALPHABETS TRACING FOR TODDLERS

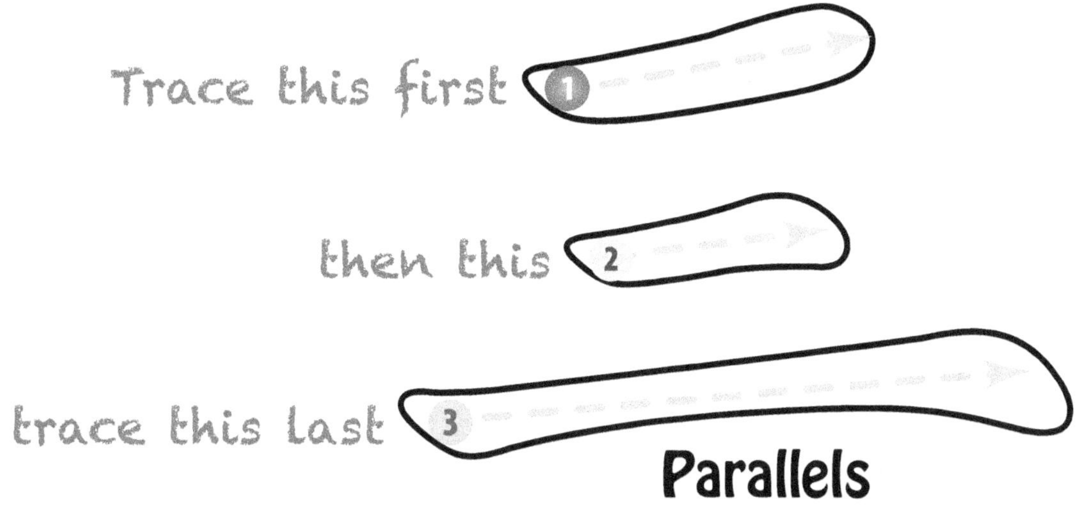

Trace this first
then this
trace this last
Parallels

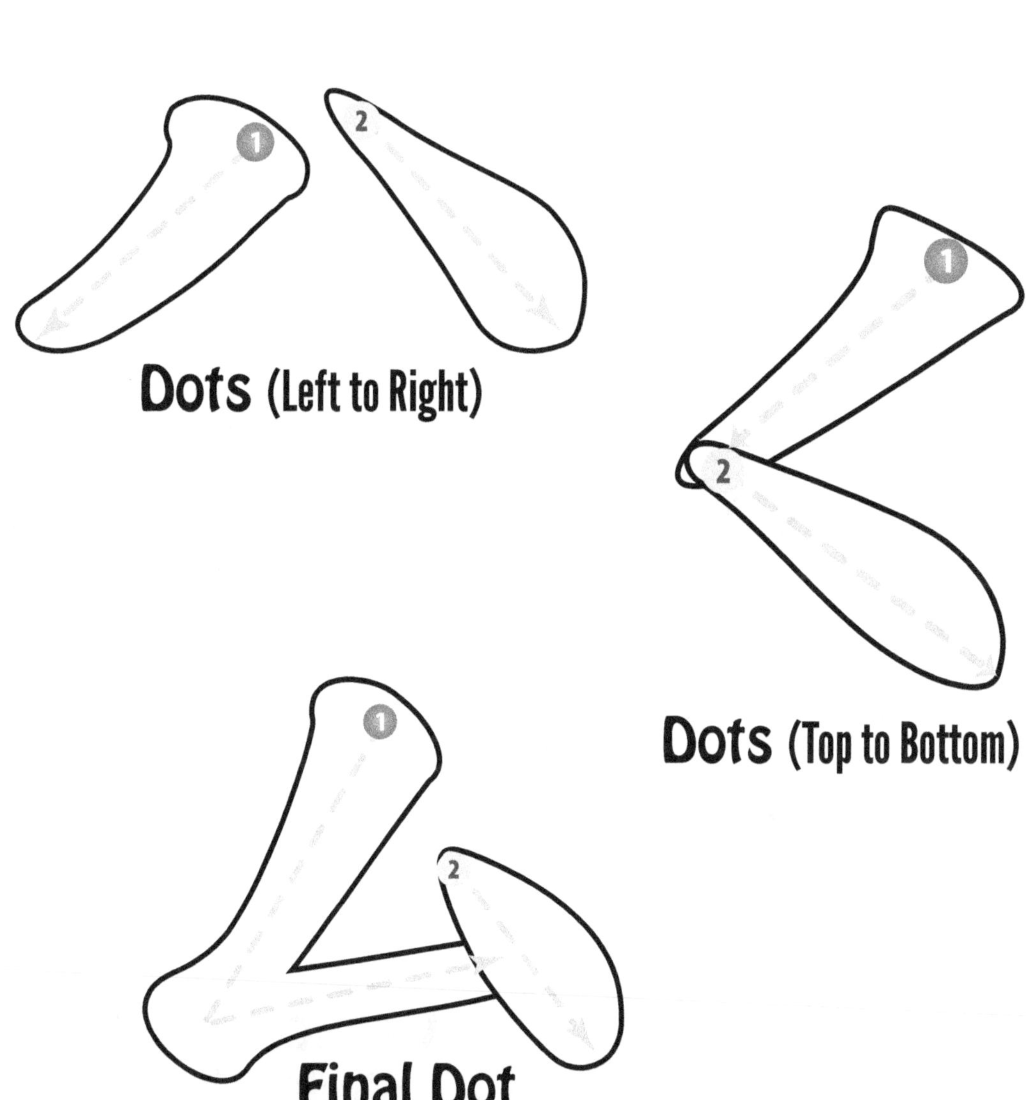

Dots (Left to Right)
Dots (Top to Bottom)
Final Dot

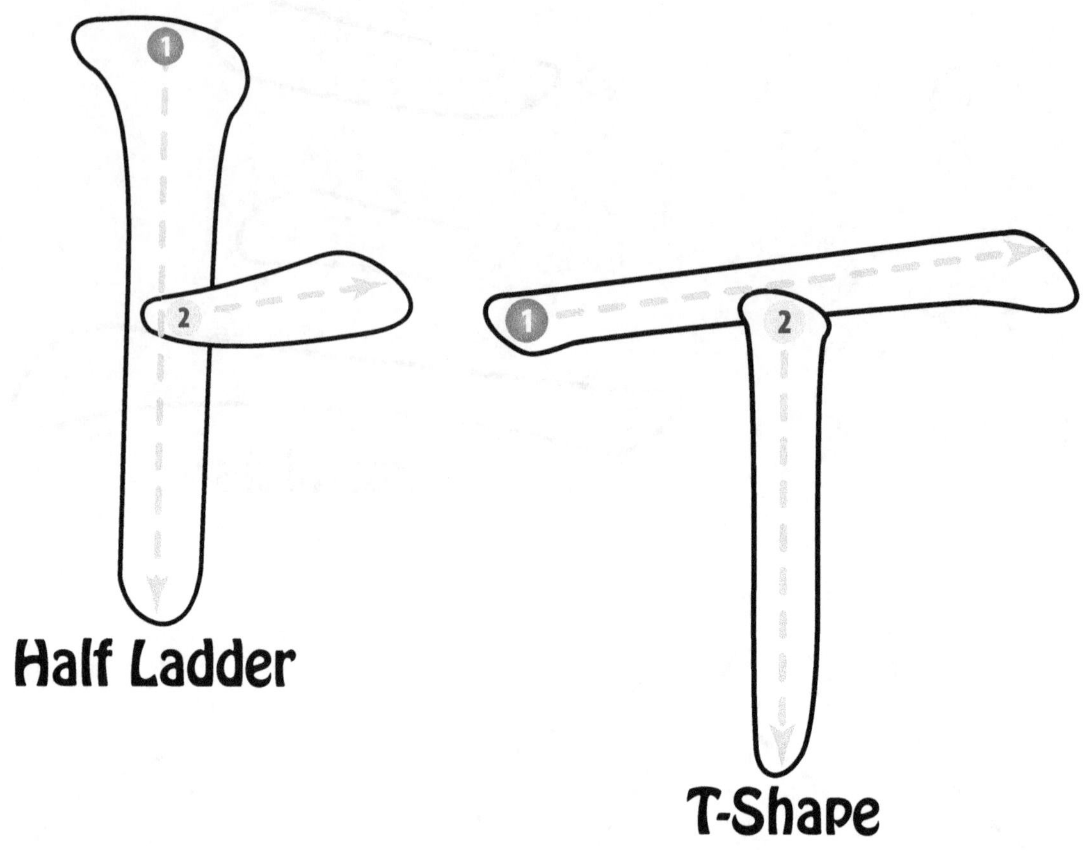

1
2
Half Ladder
1
2
T-Shape

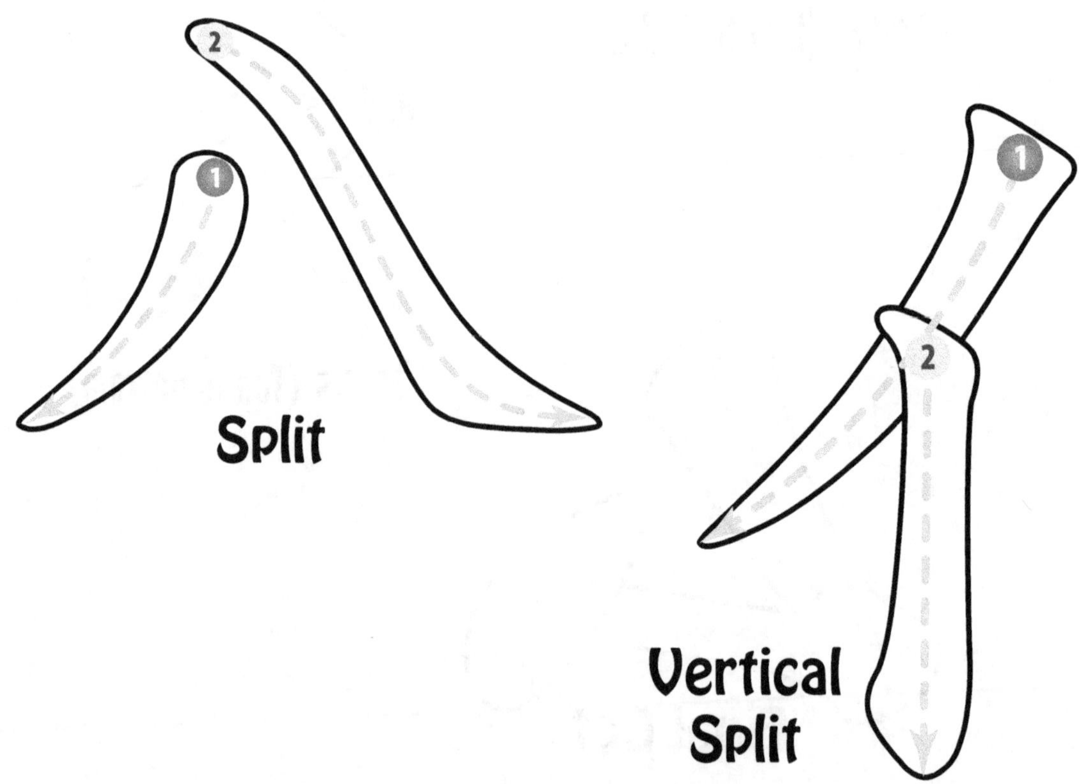

2
1
Split
1
2
Vertical
Split

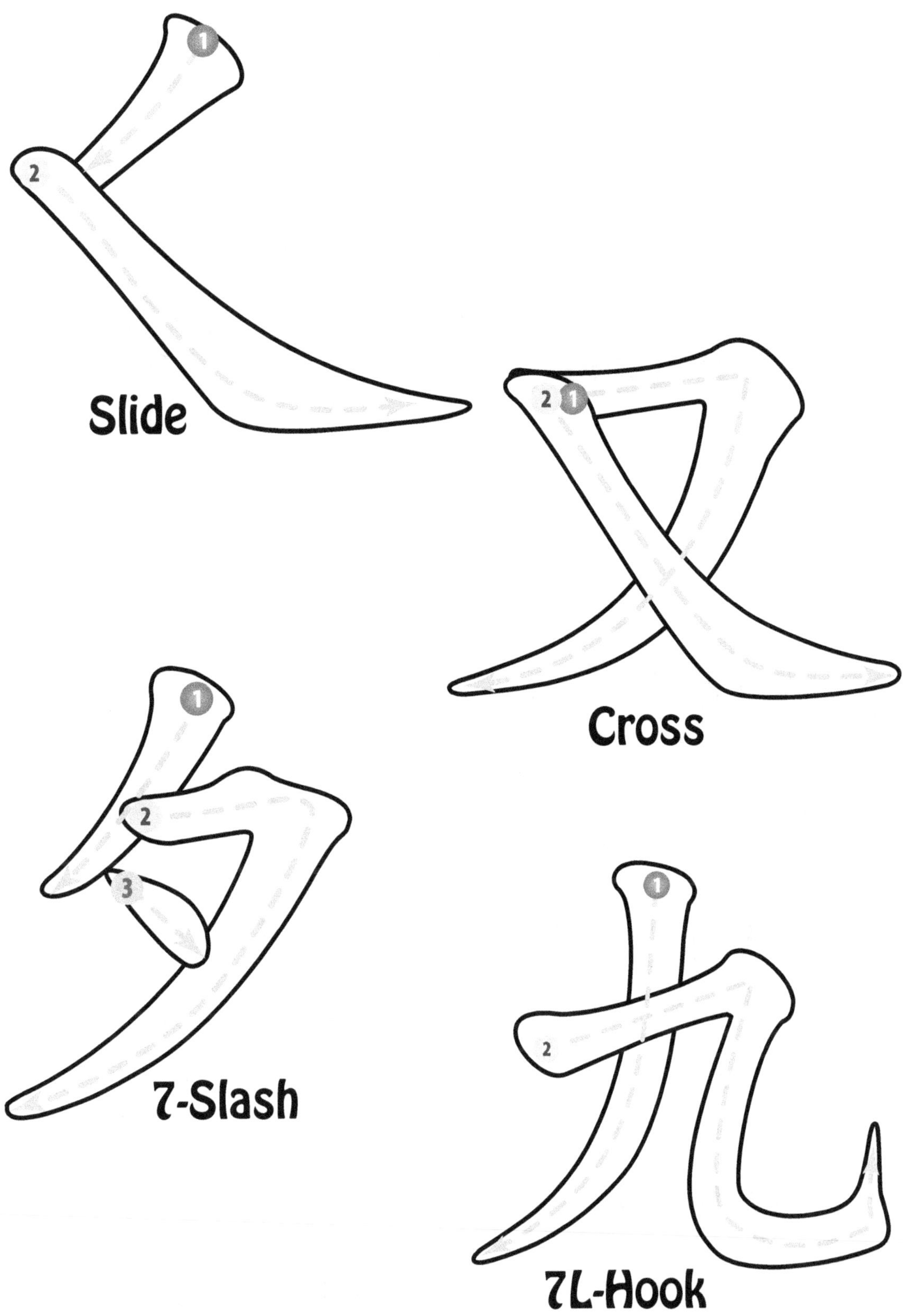
Slide
Cross
7-Slash
7L-Hook

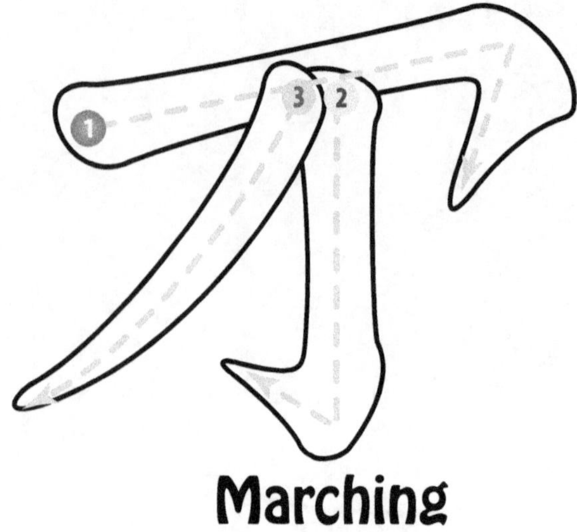

Marching

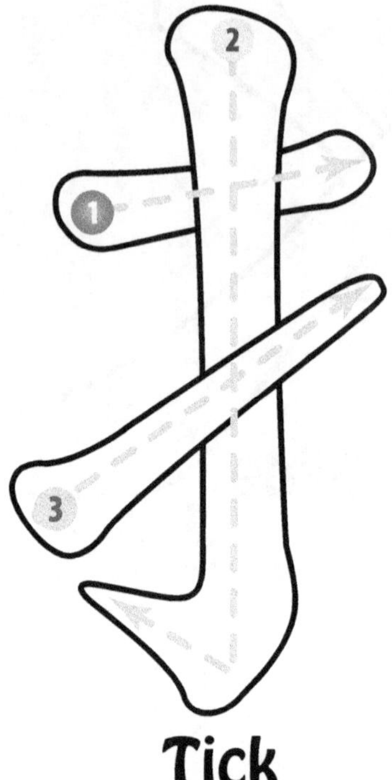

Tick

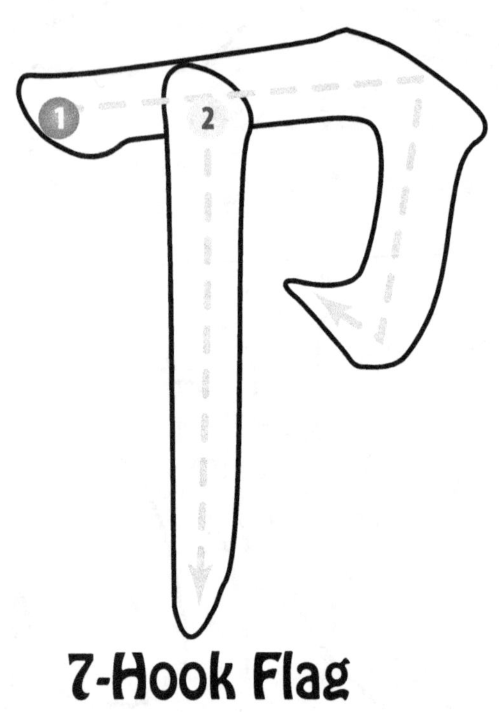

7-Hook Flag

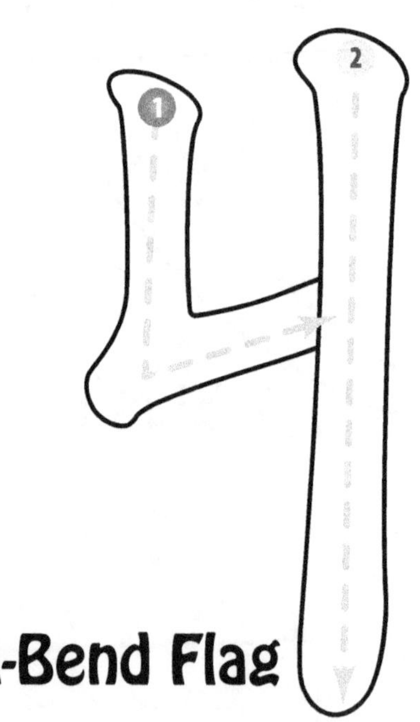

L-Bend Flag

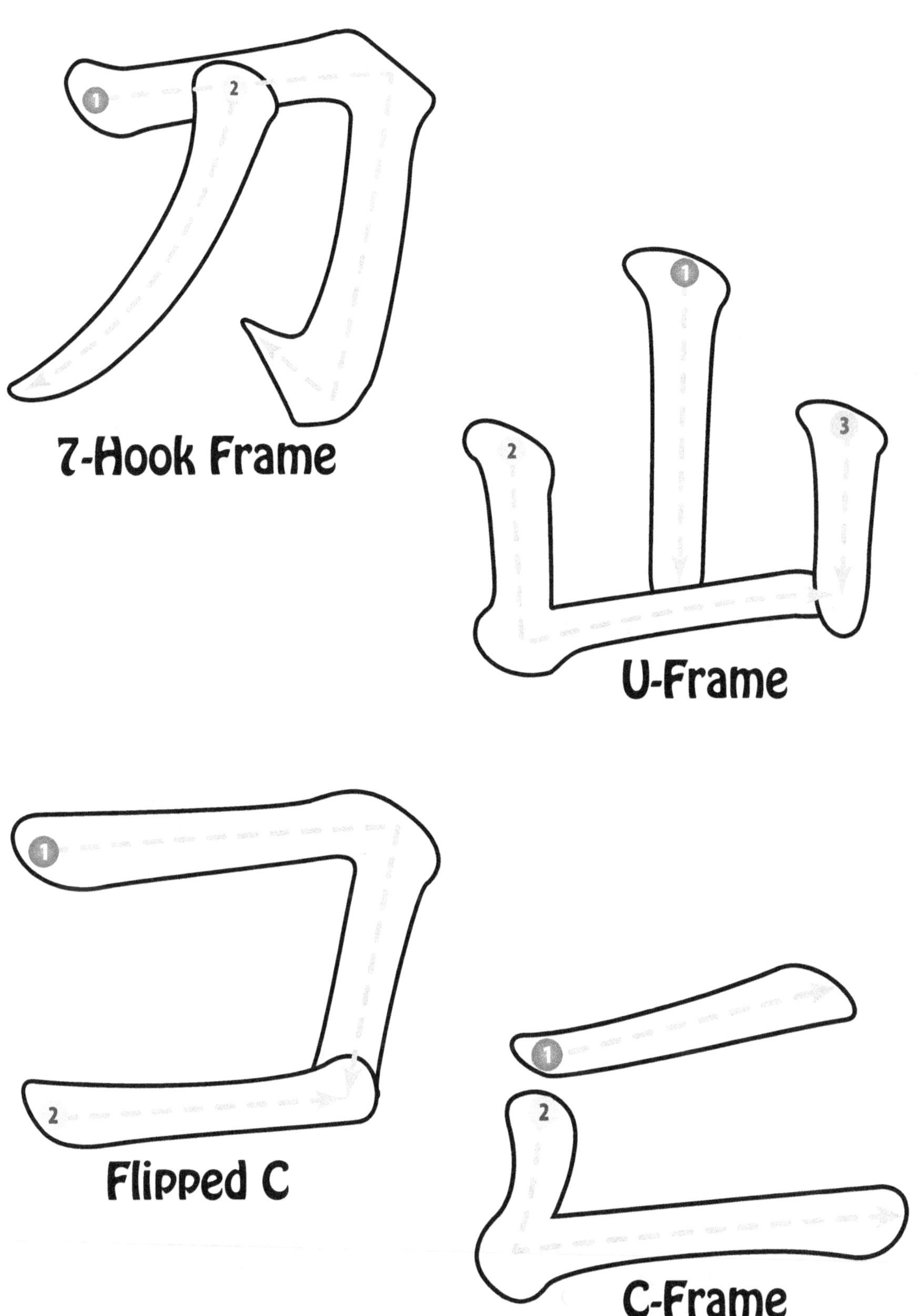

7-Hook Frame
U-Frame
Flipped C
C-Frame

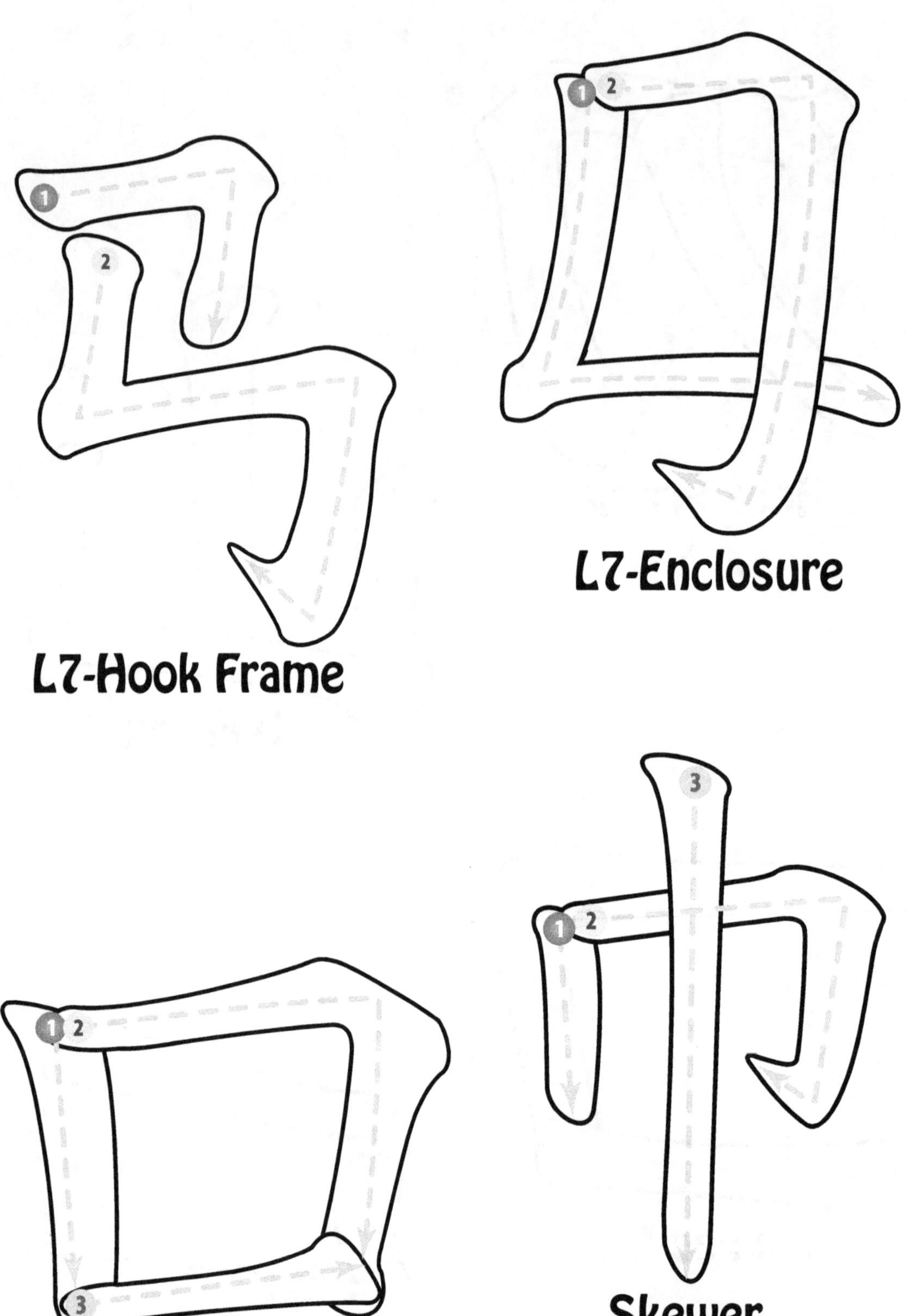

1
2
L7-Hook Frame
1 2
L7-Enclosure
1 2
3
n-Frame
3
Skewer

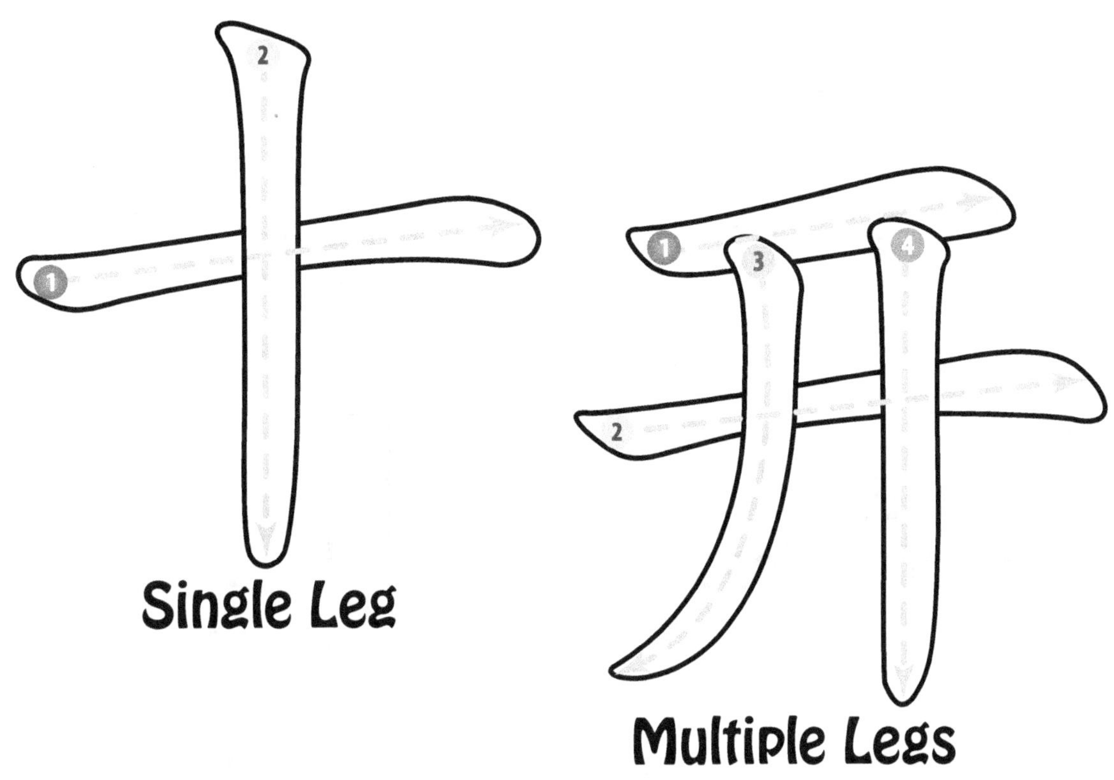

Single Leg

Multiple Legs

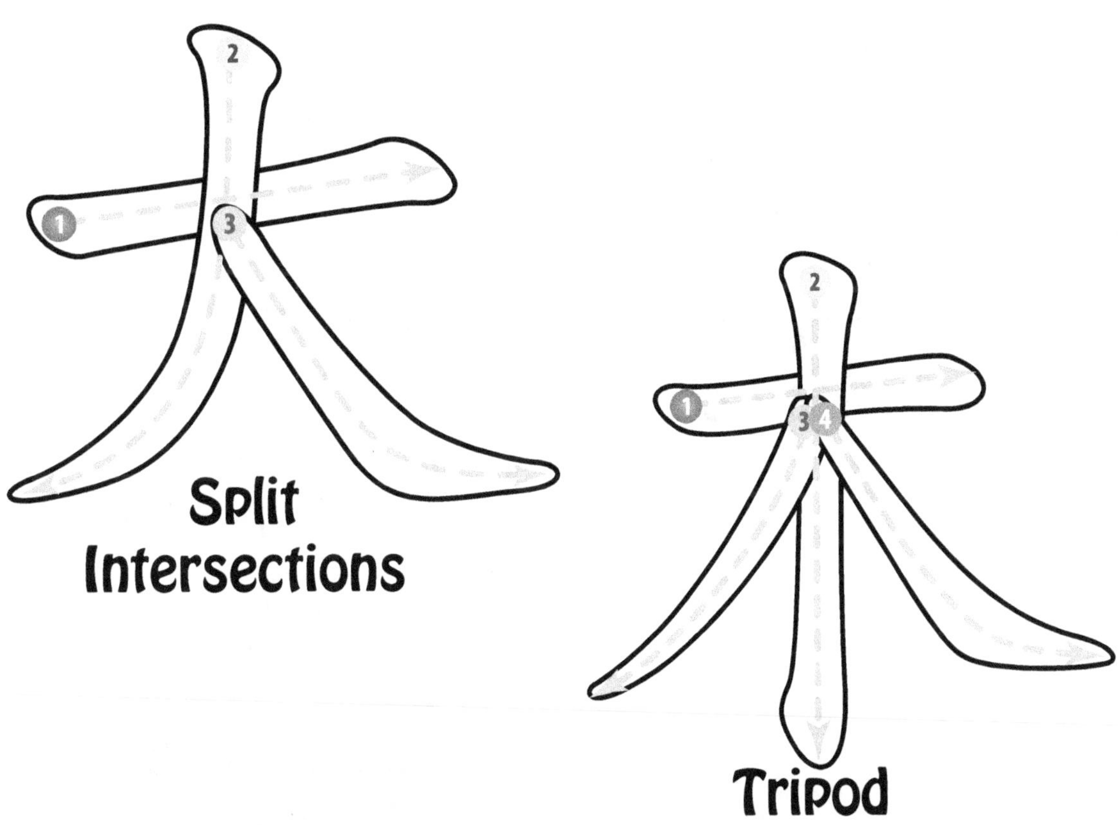

Split Intersections

Tripod

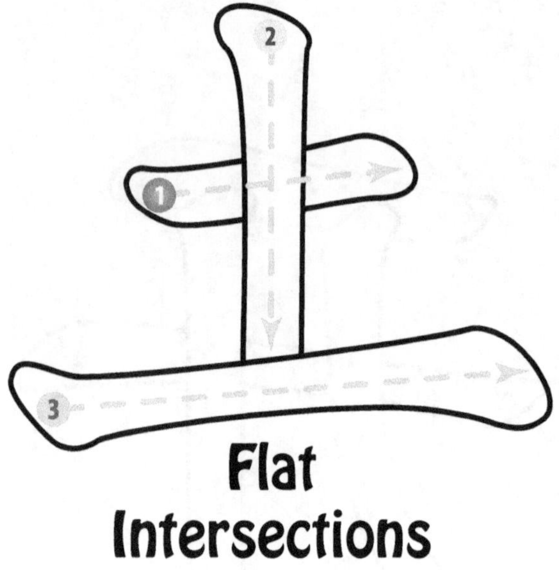

**Flat
Intersections**

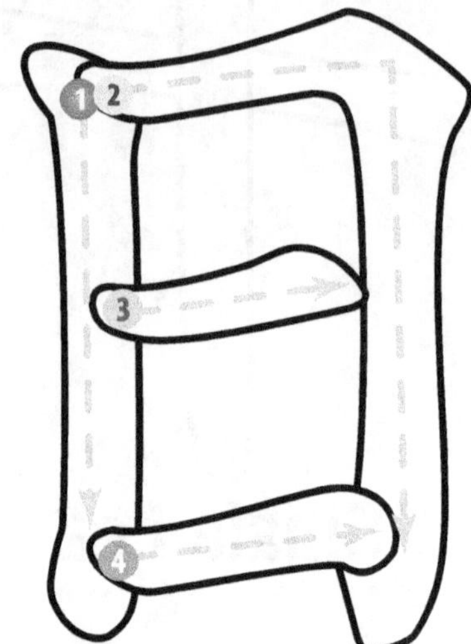

**Horizontals
Enclosure**

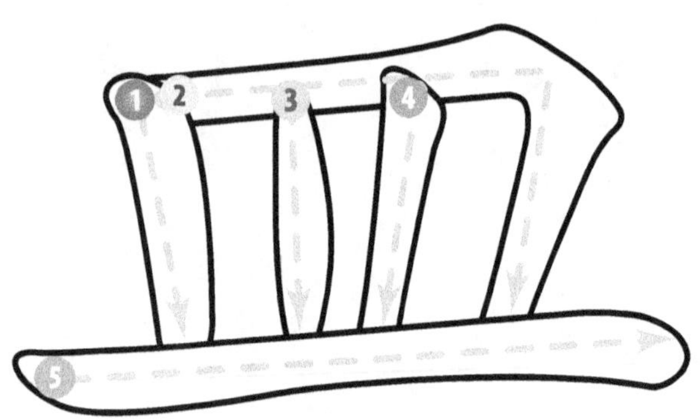

**Verticals
Enclosure**

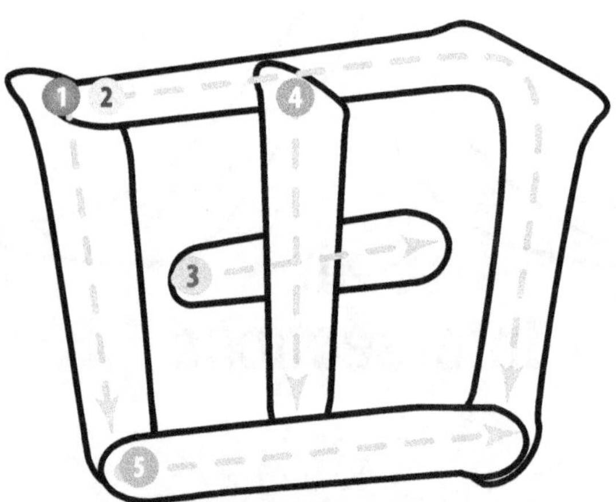

**Intersections
Enclosure**

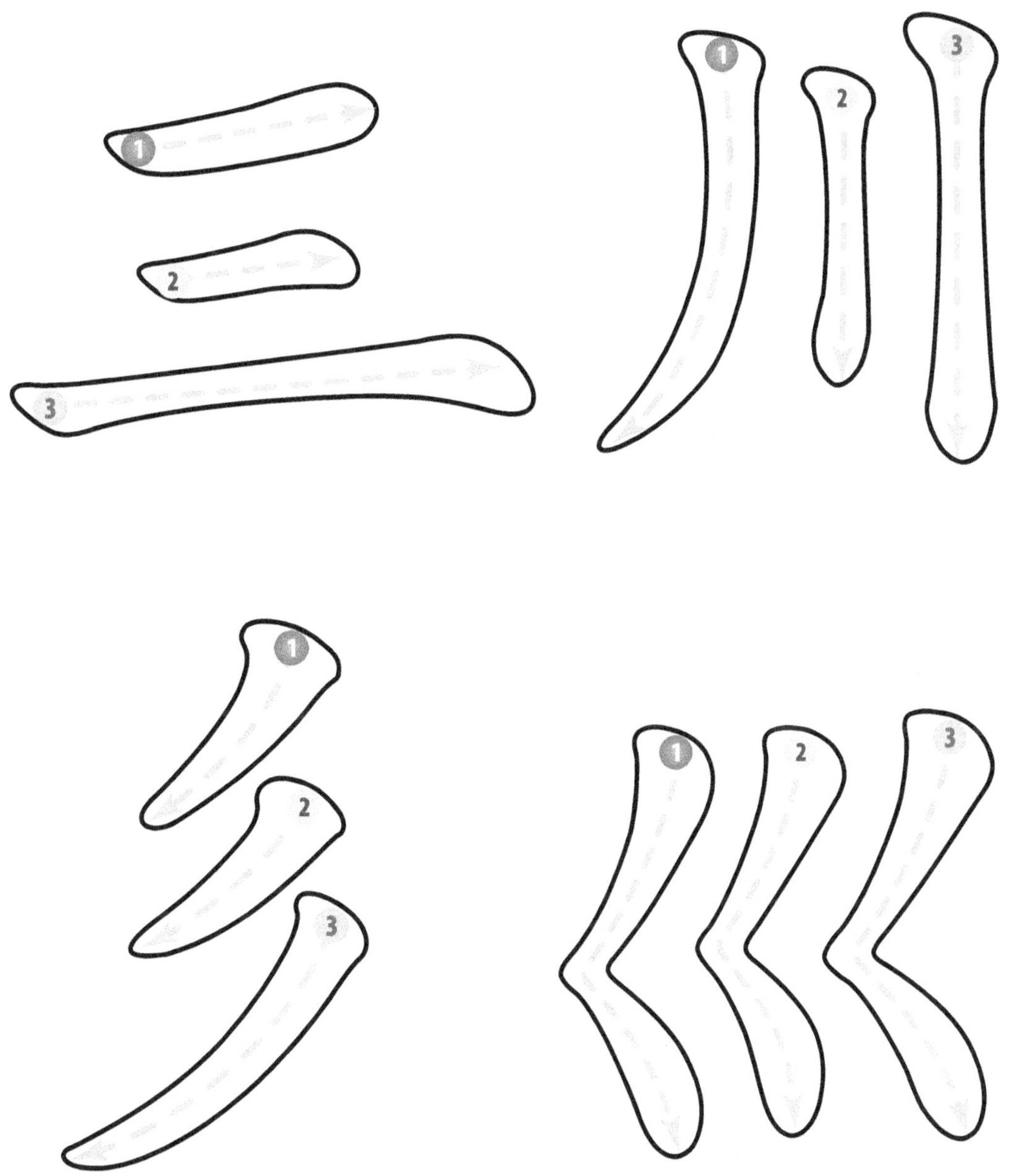

Dots (Left to Right)

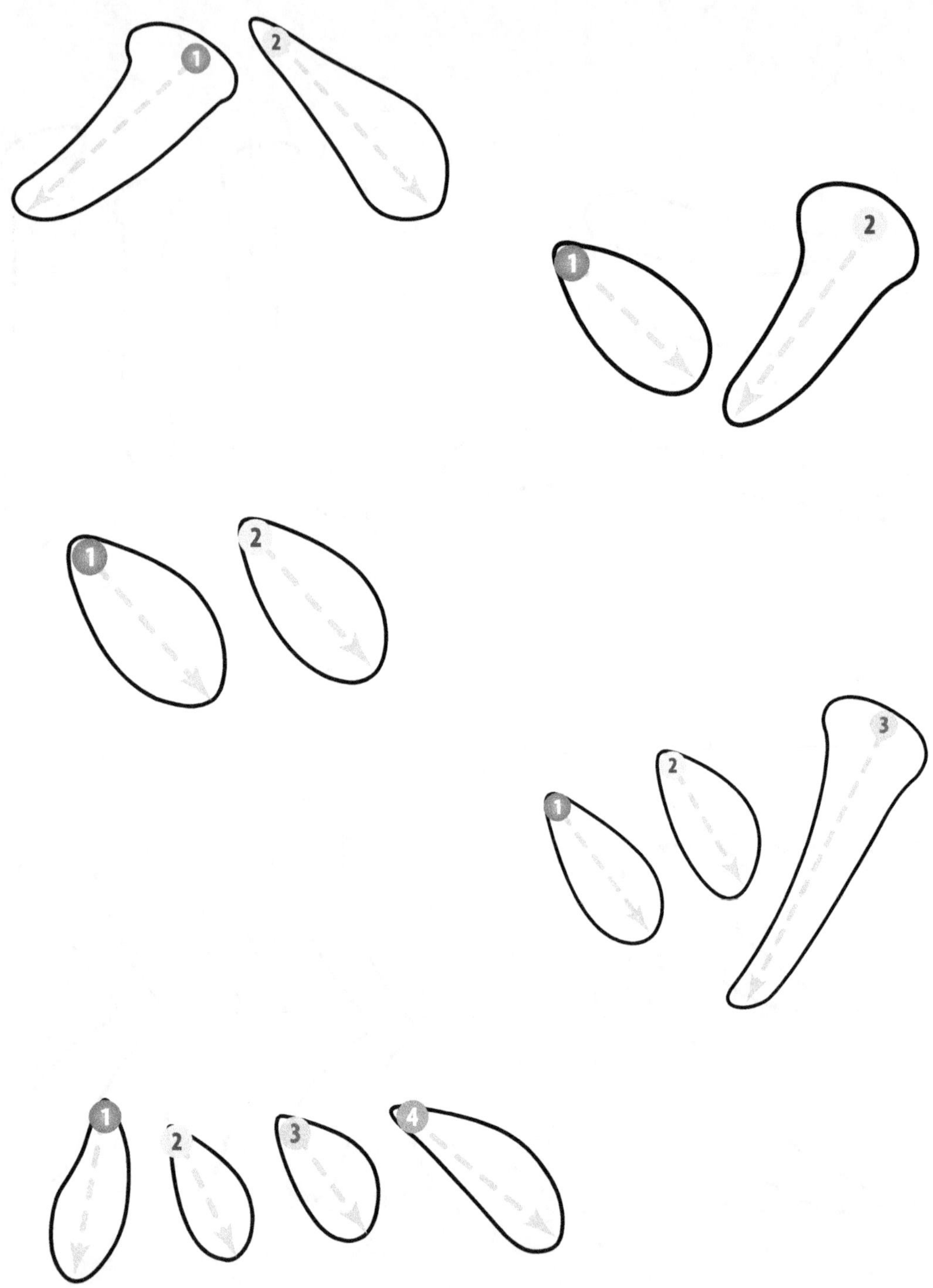

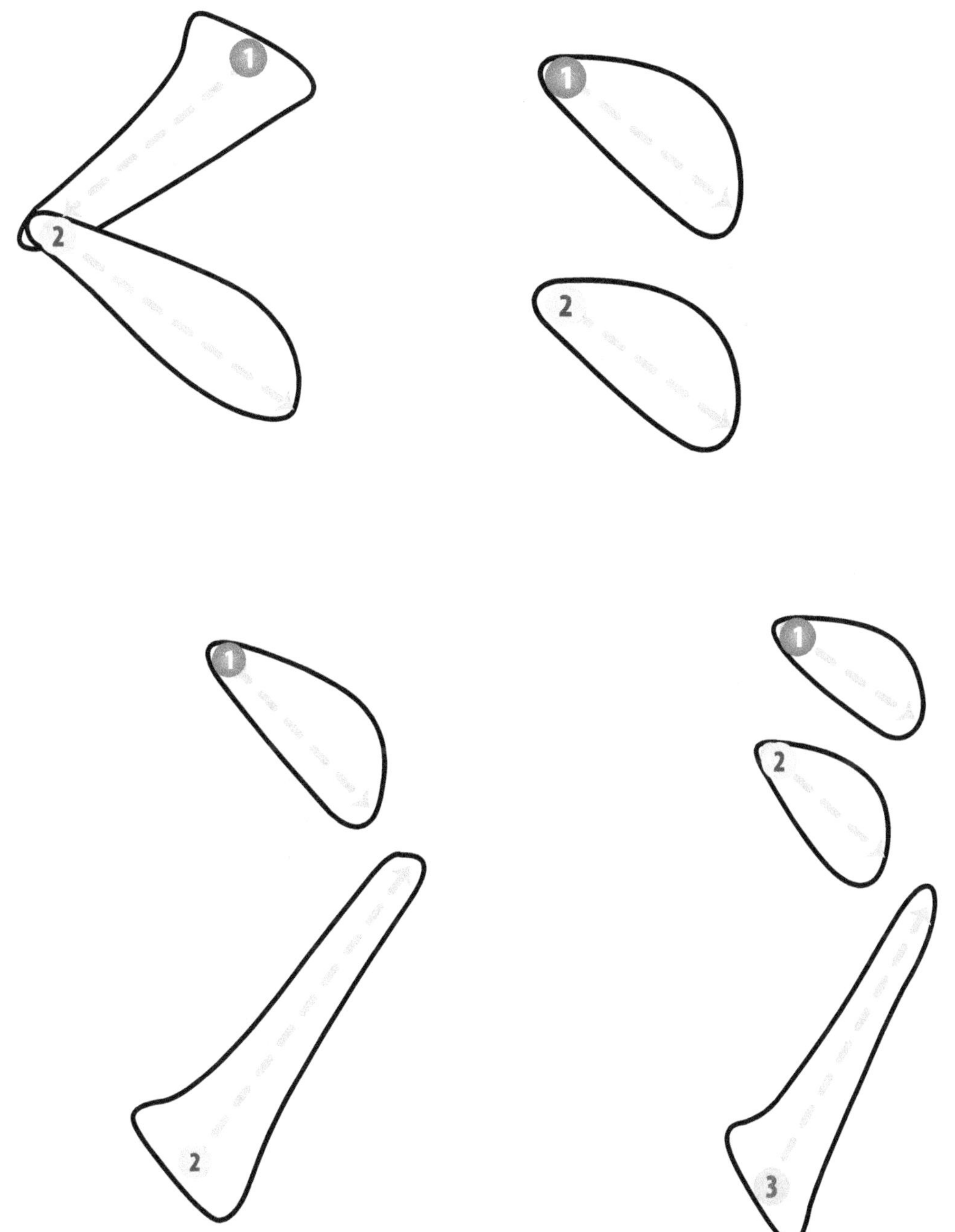

Final Dot

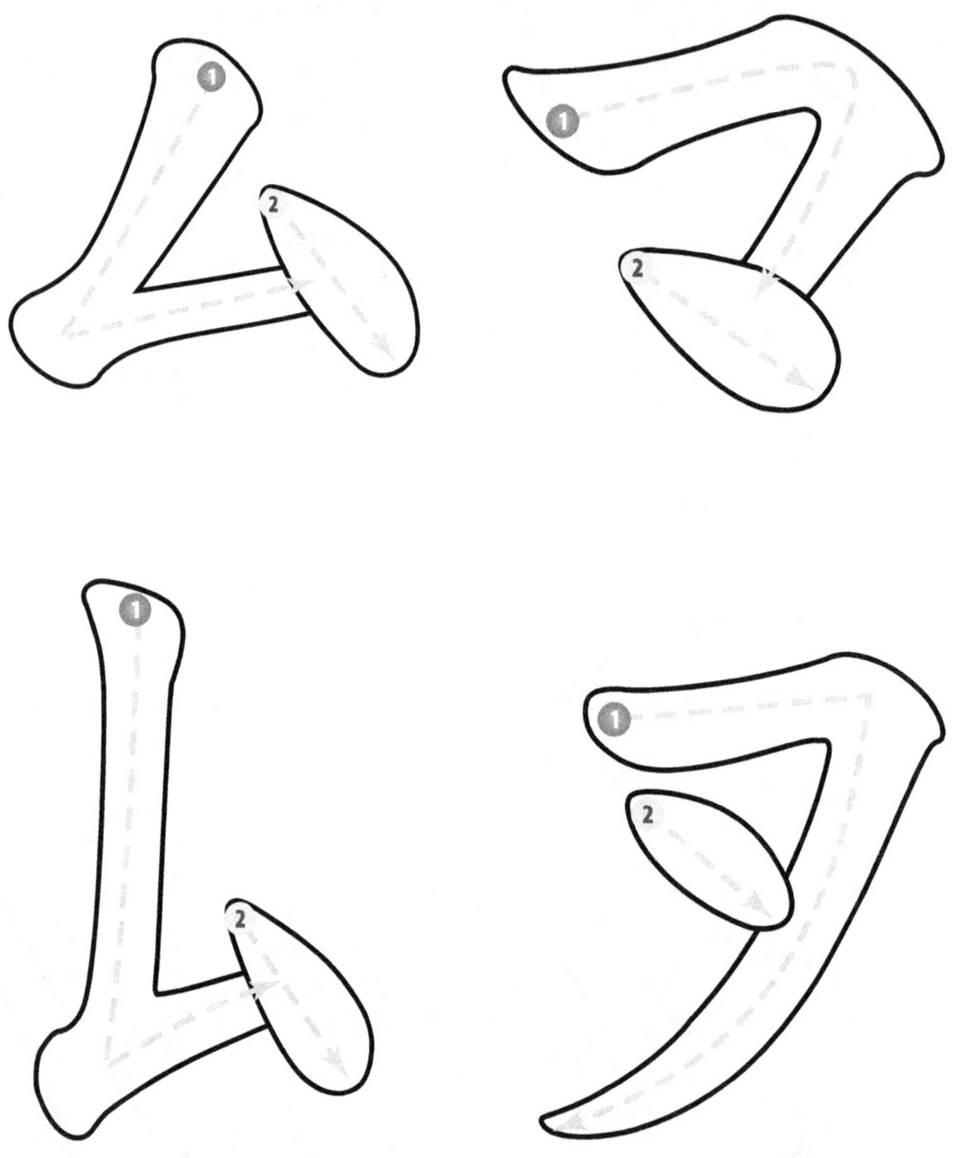

T-Shape

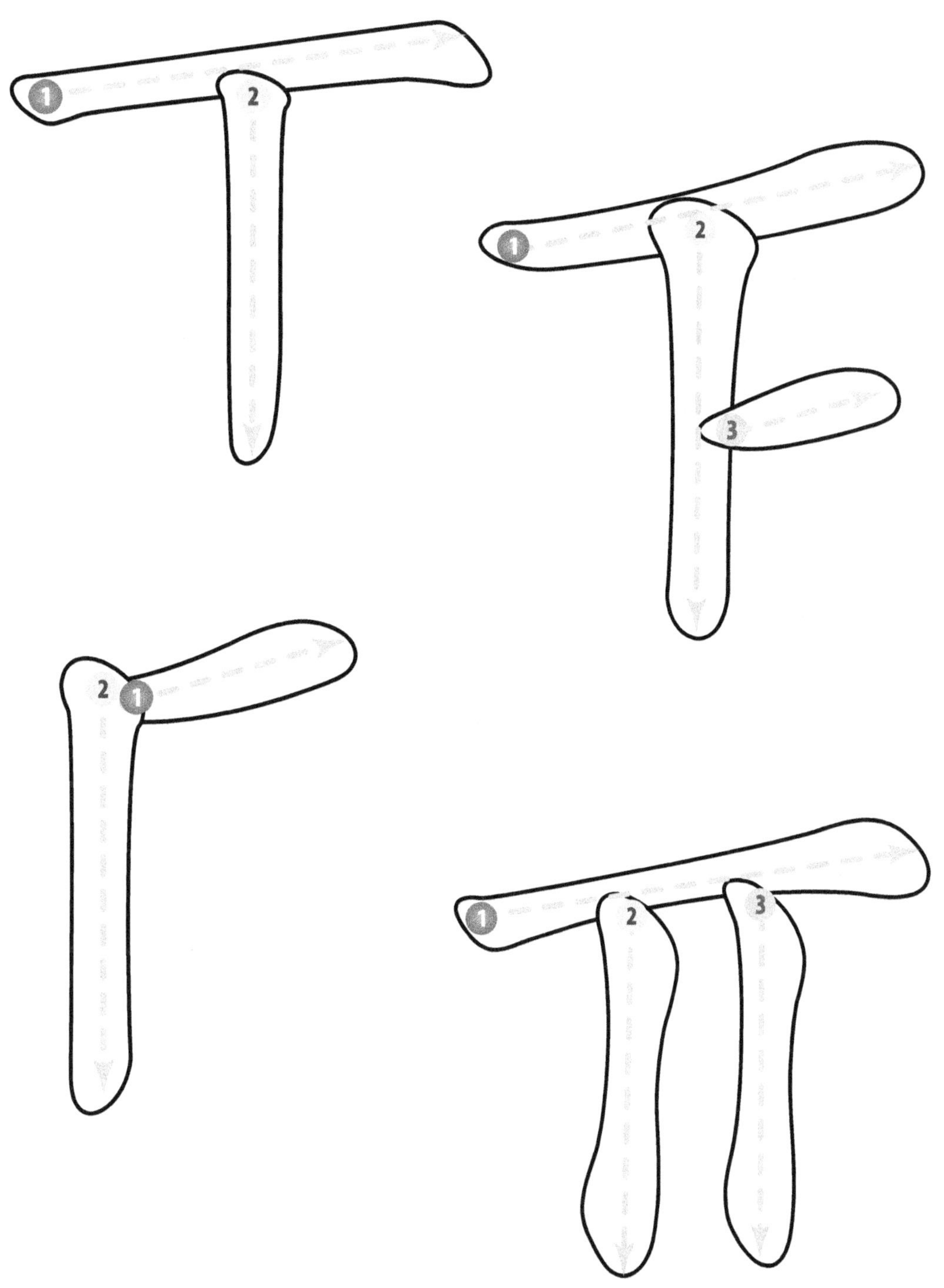

T-Shape   Half Ladder

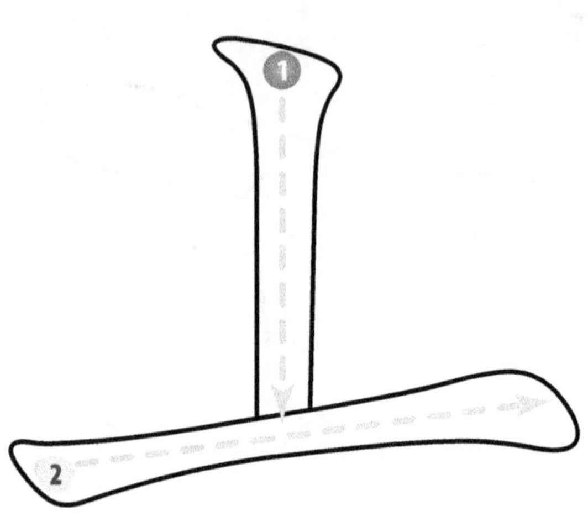

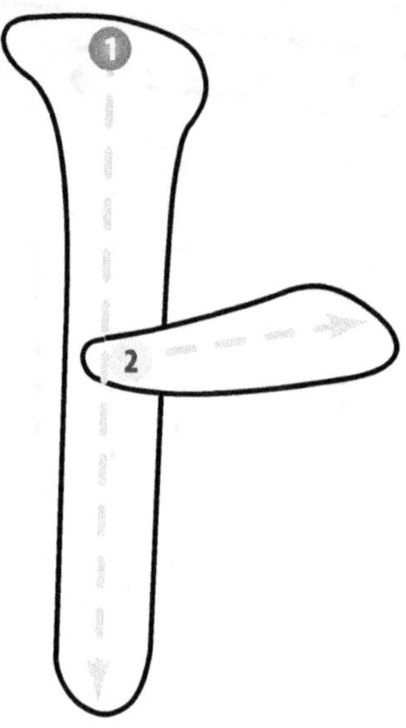

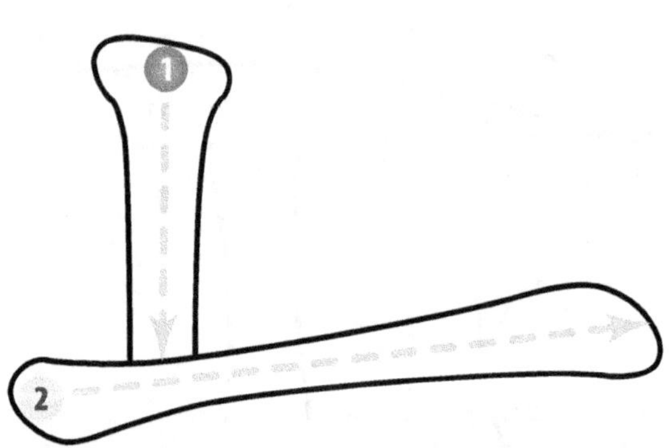

Half Ladder

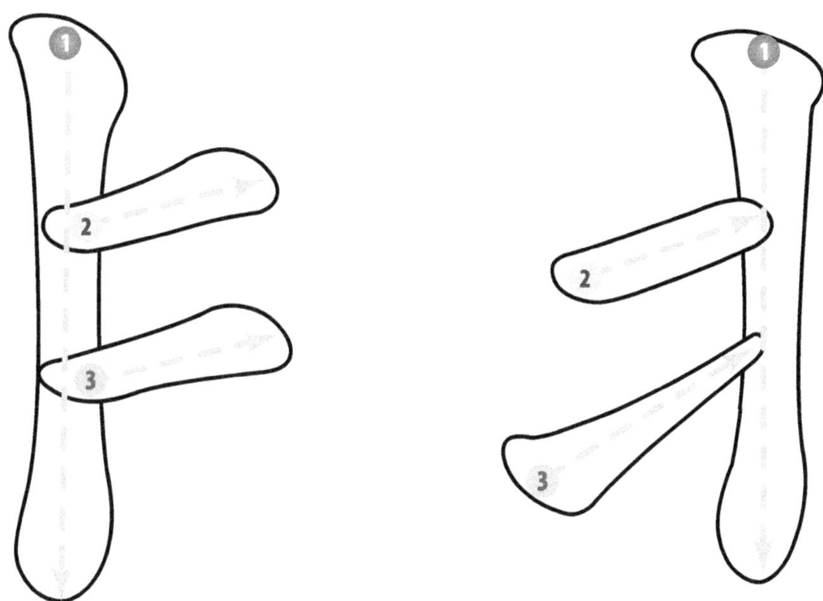

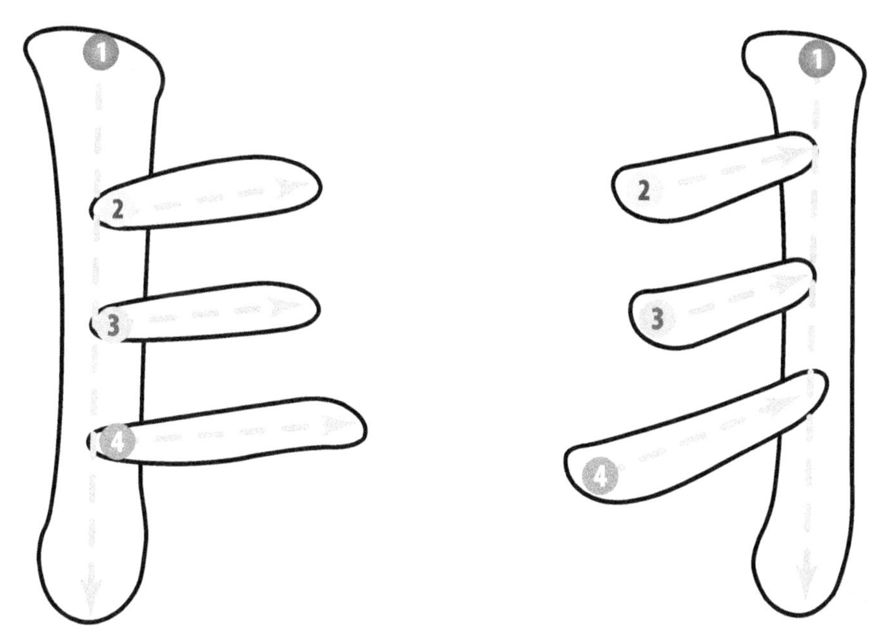

Split

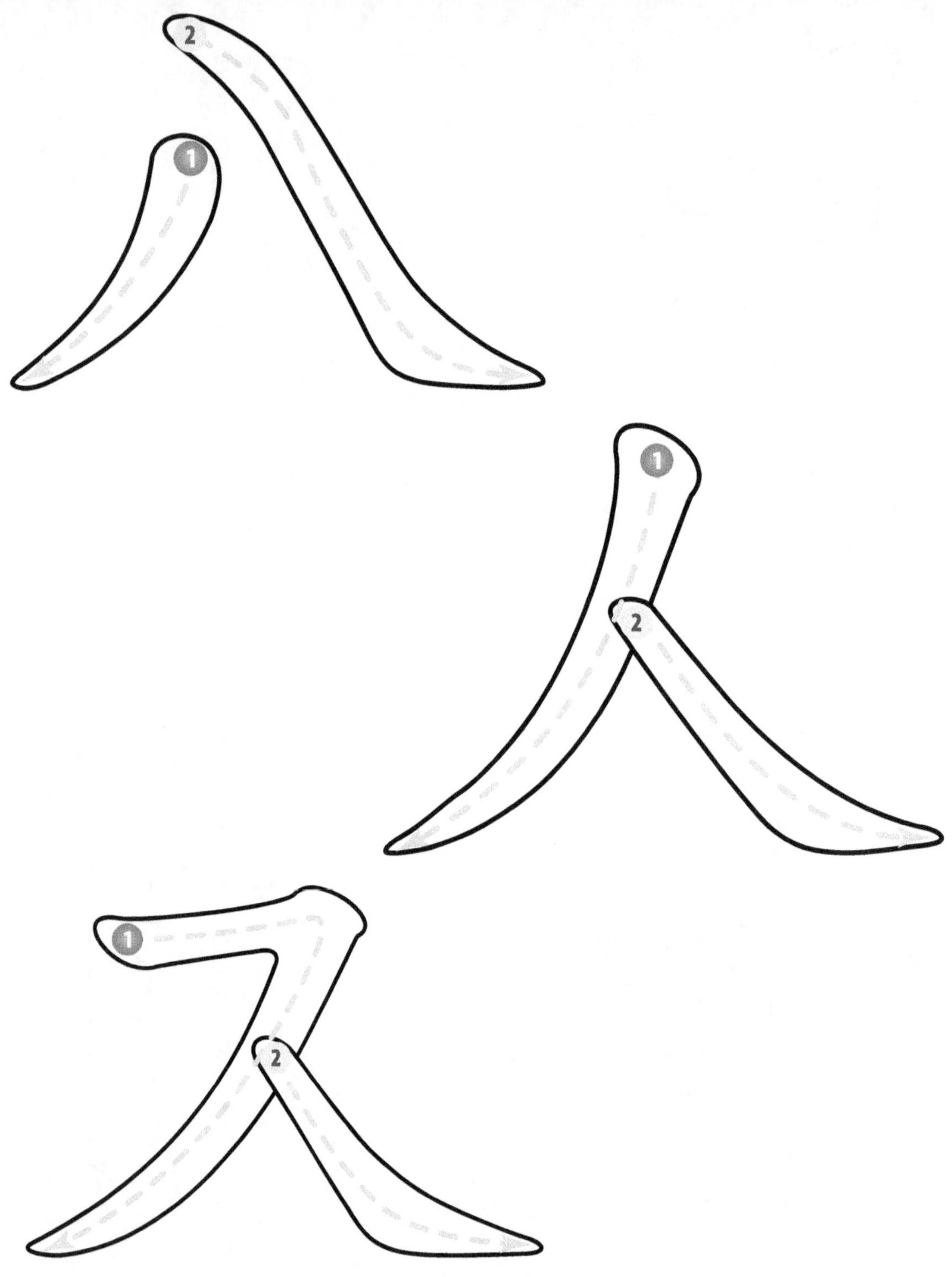

Split

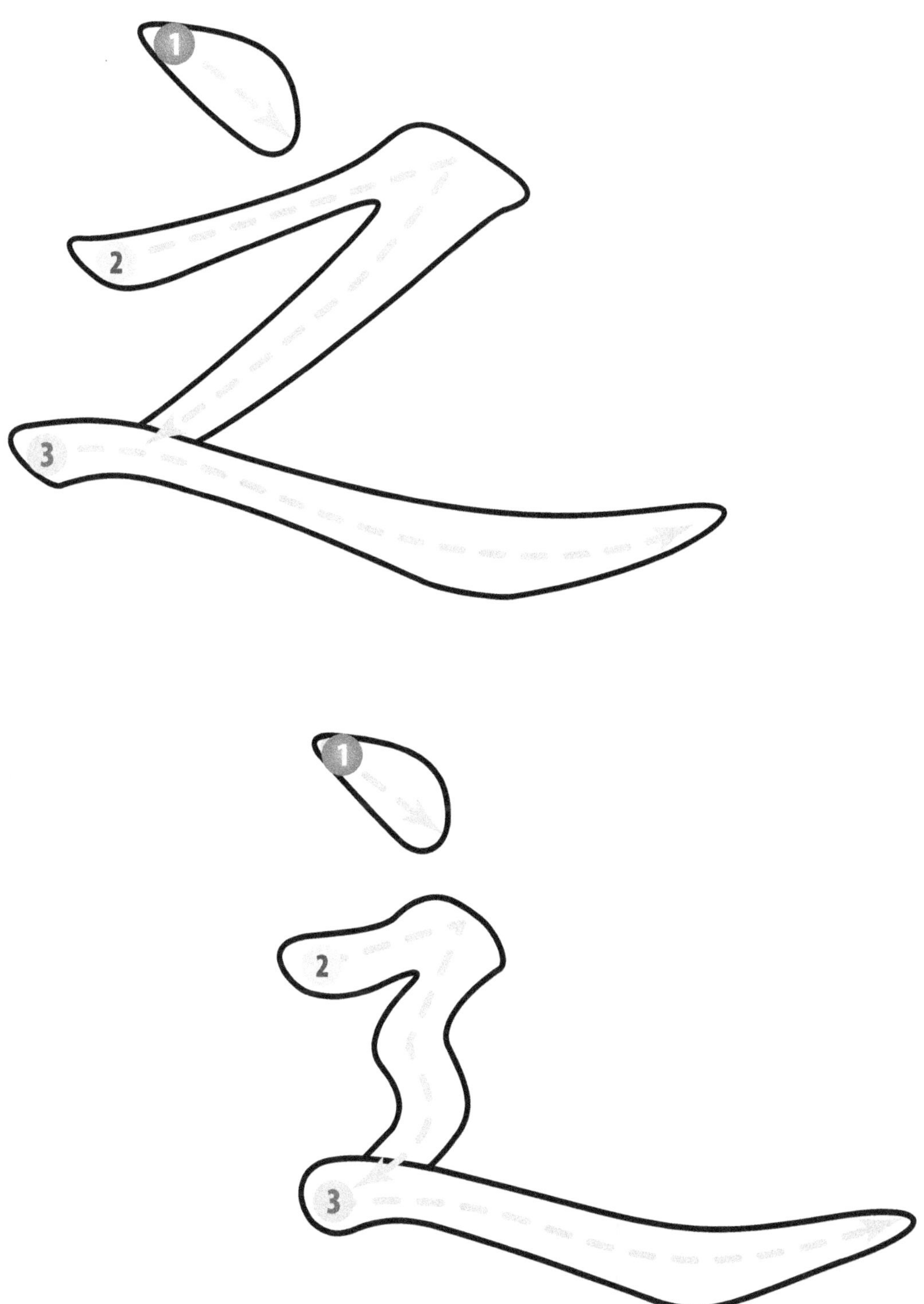

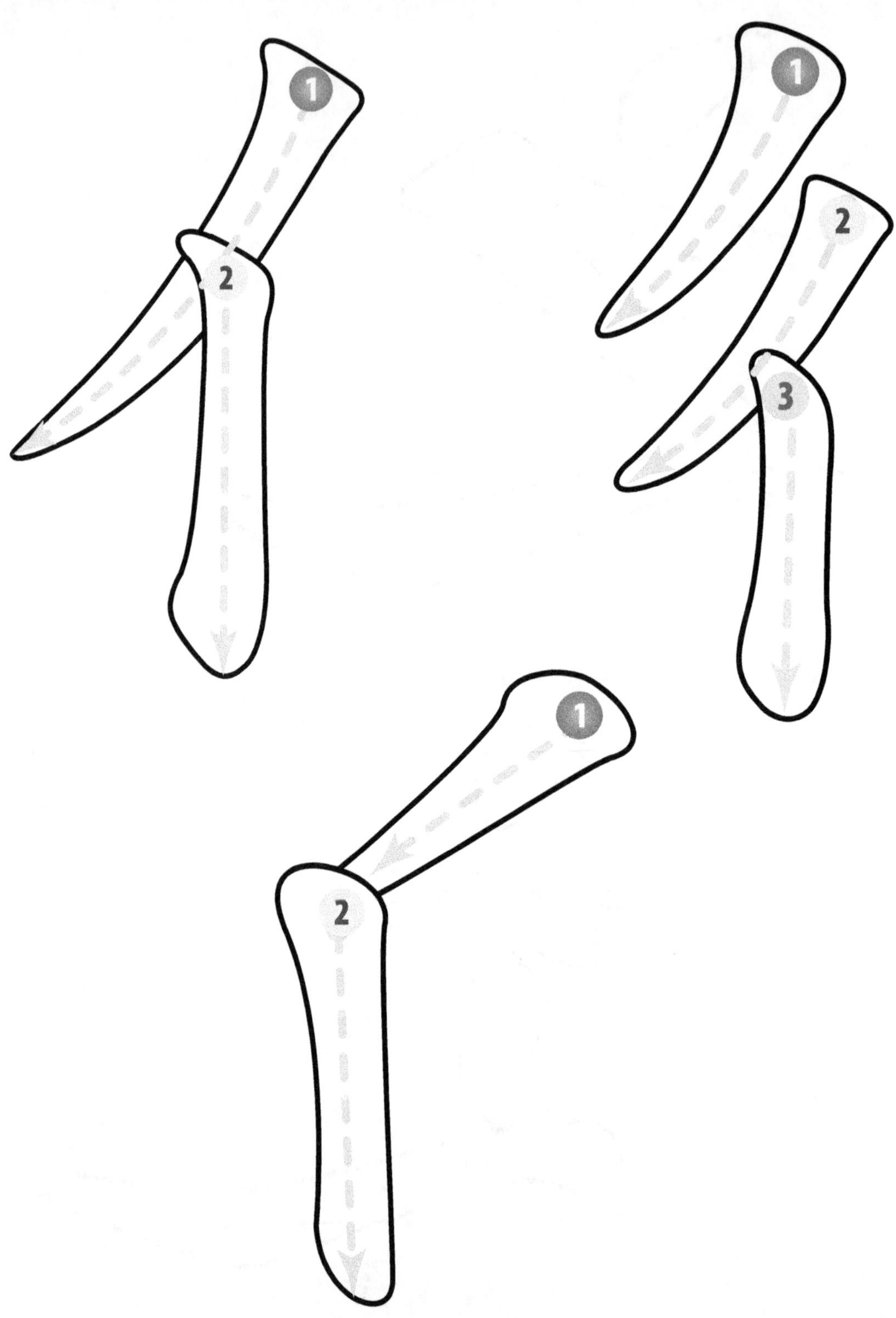

Horizontal Split

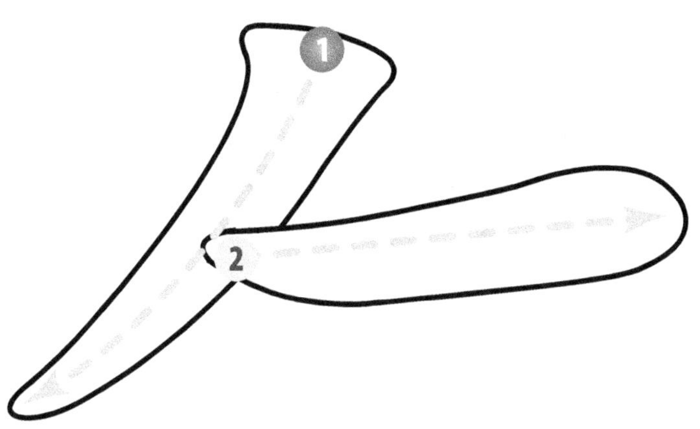

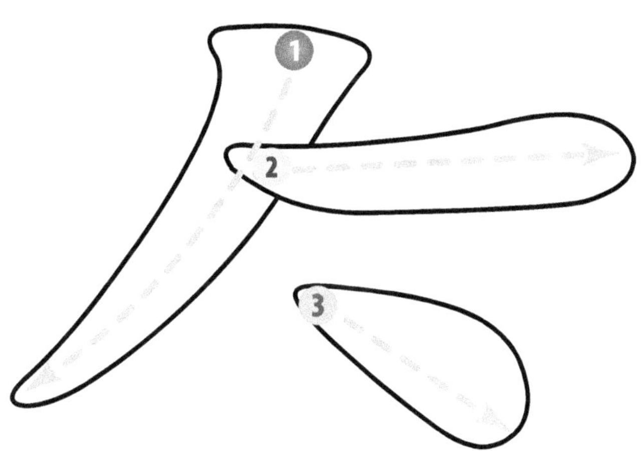

Slide

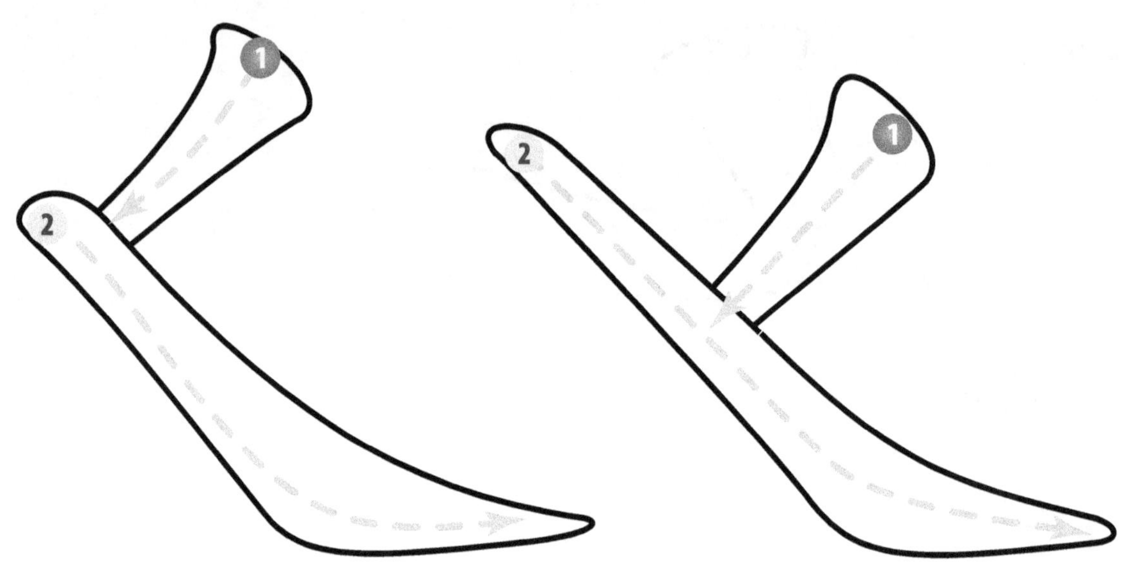

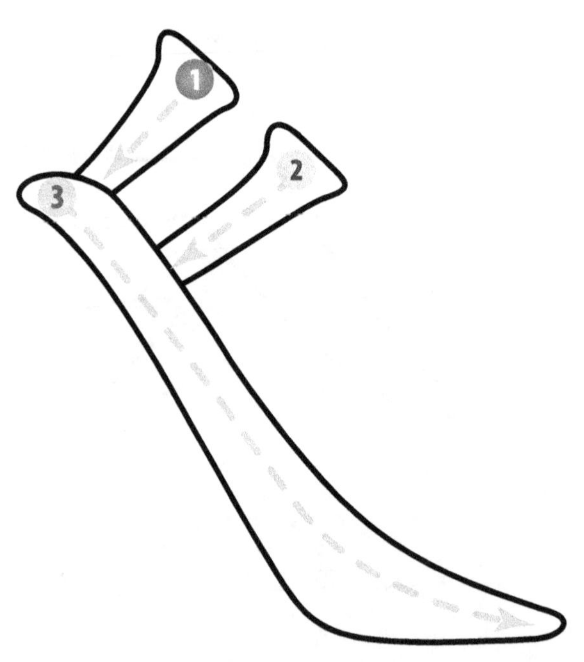

7-Slash

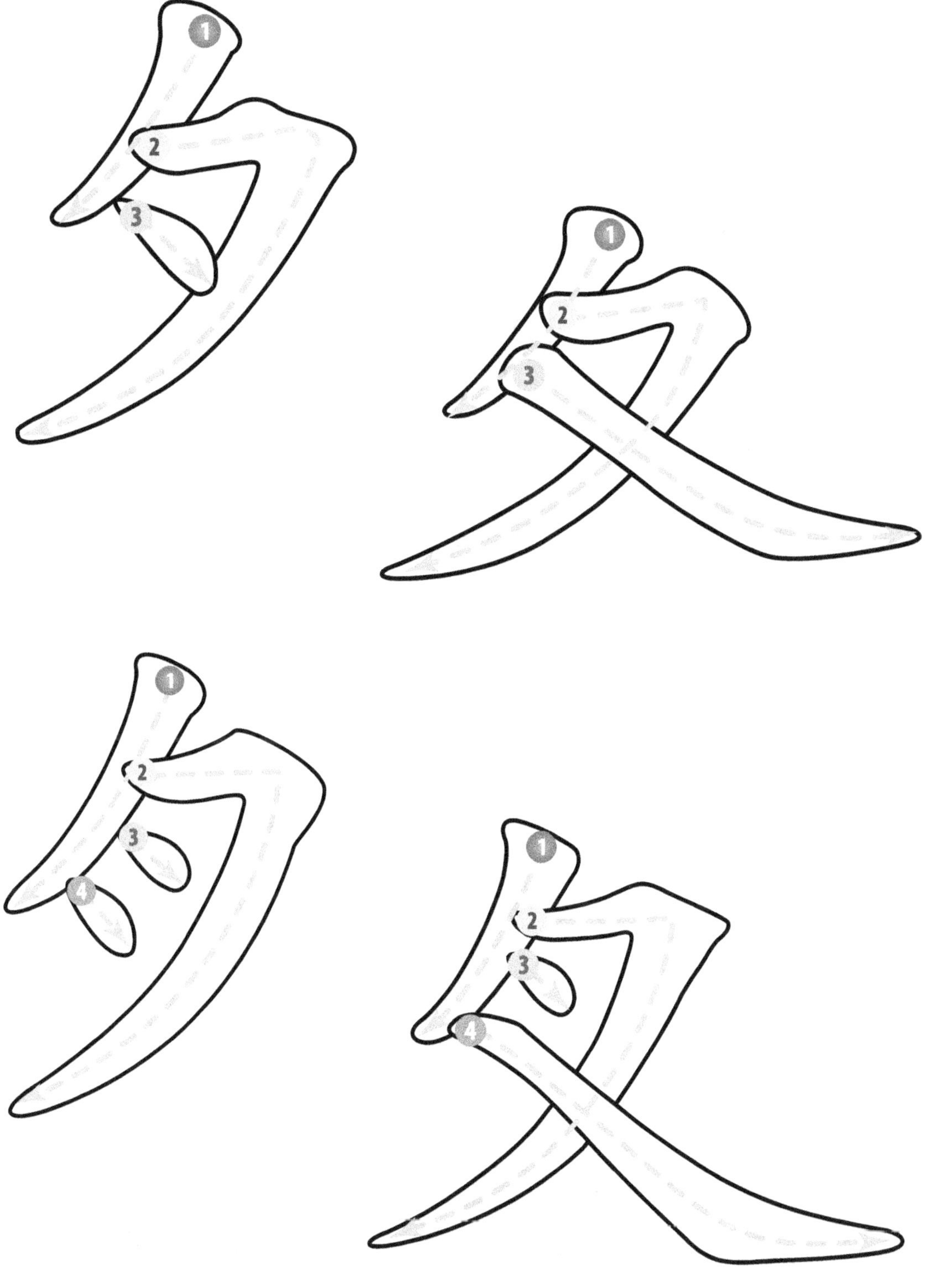

儿-Hook

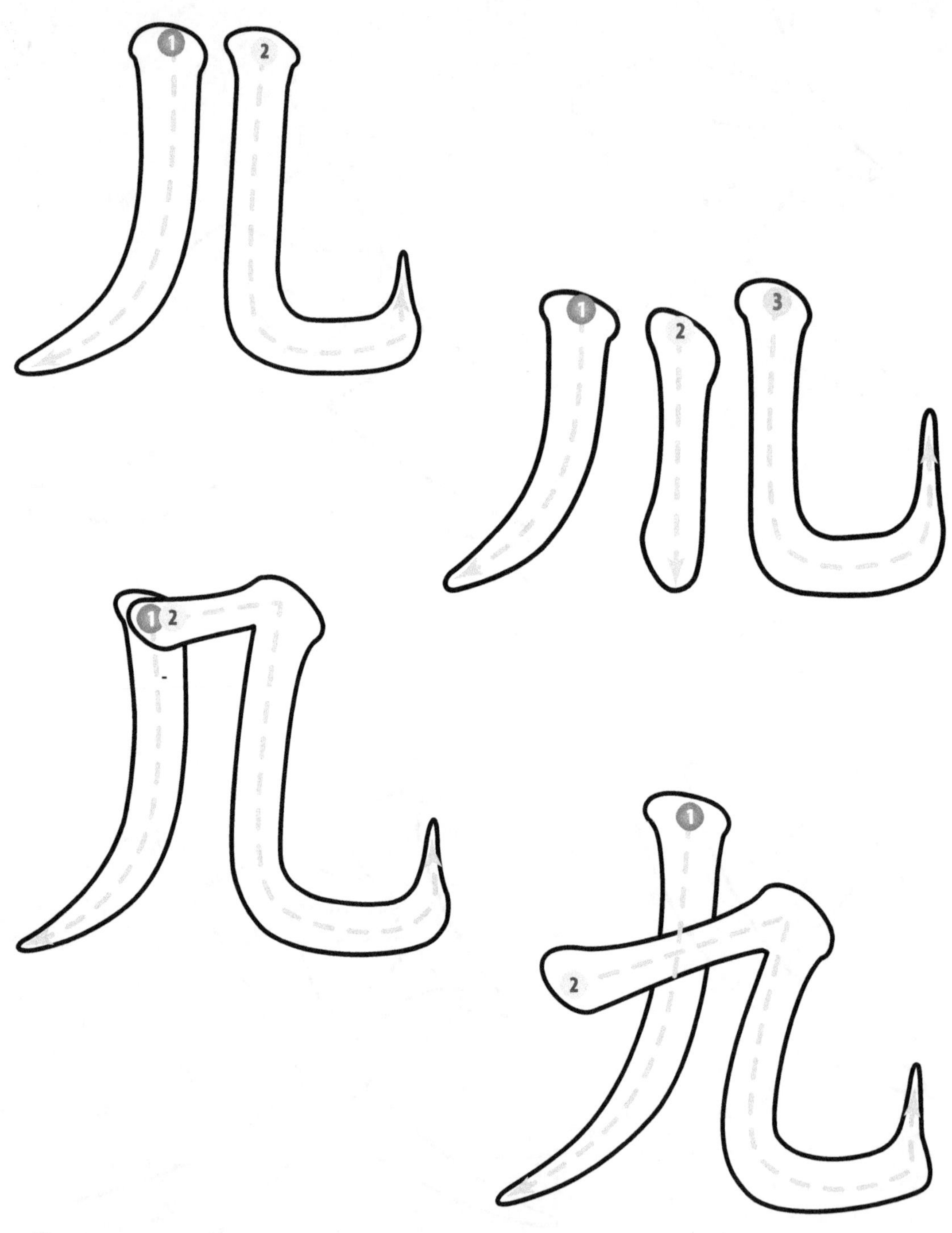

Cross

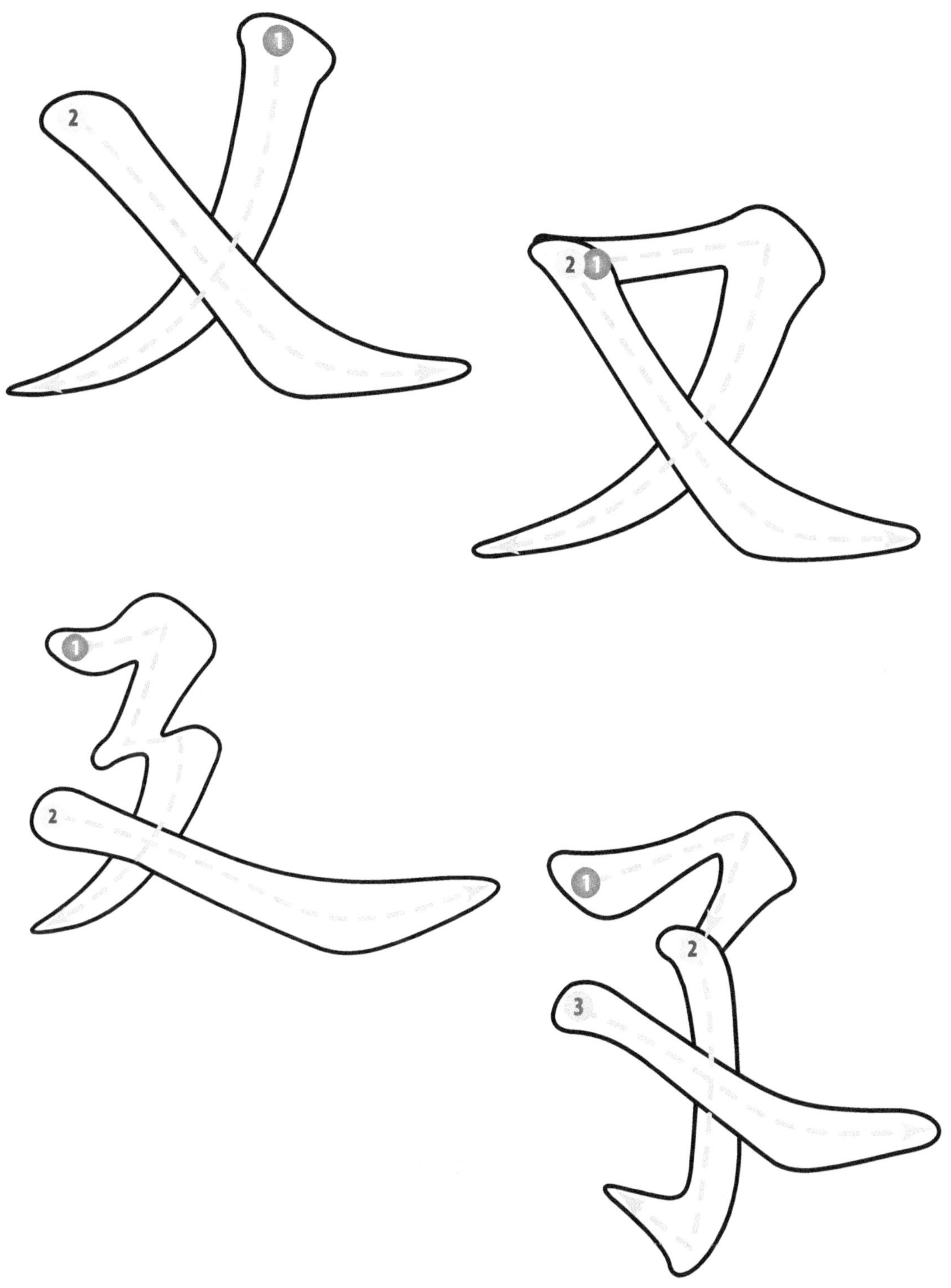

Marching

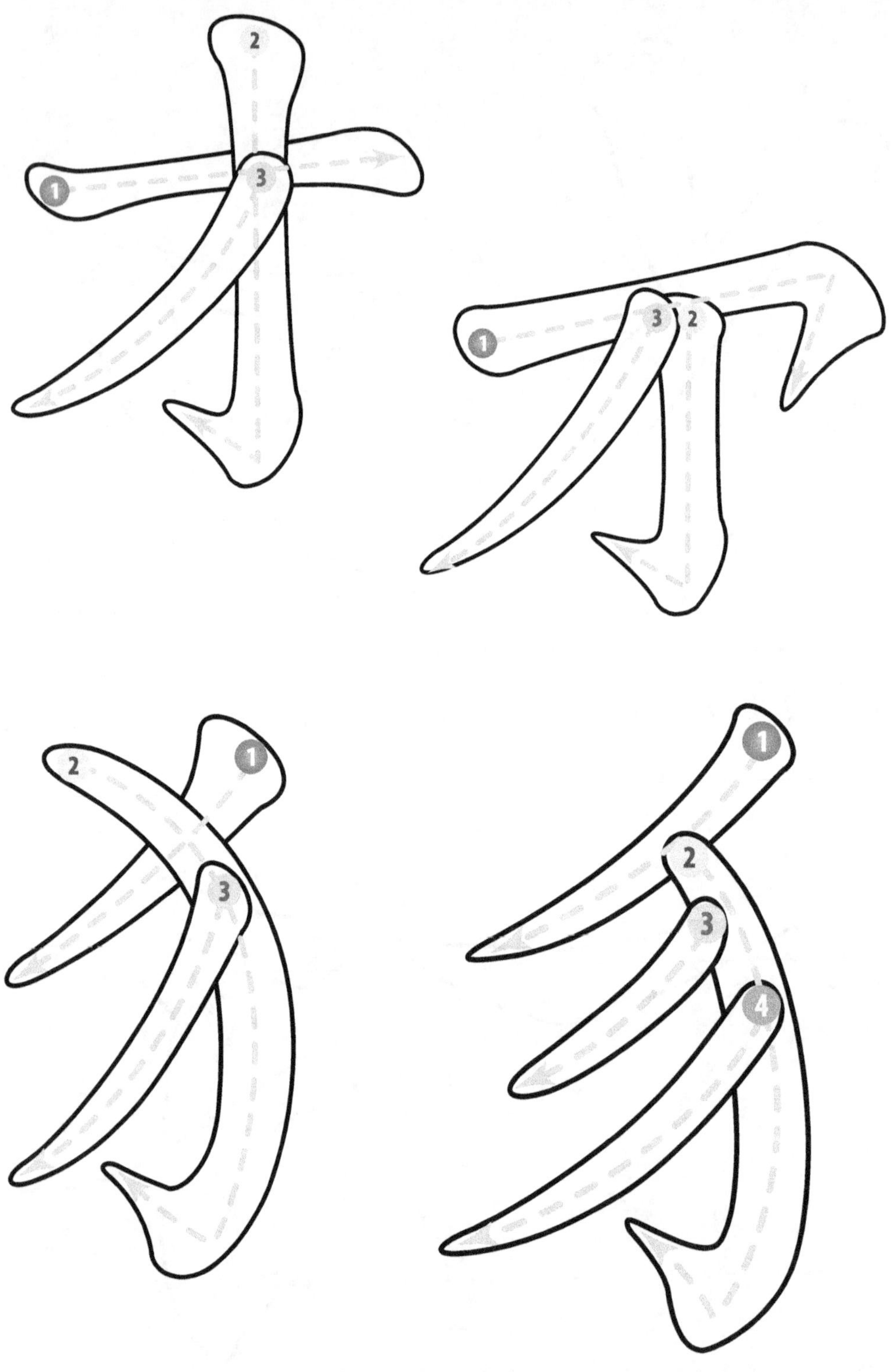

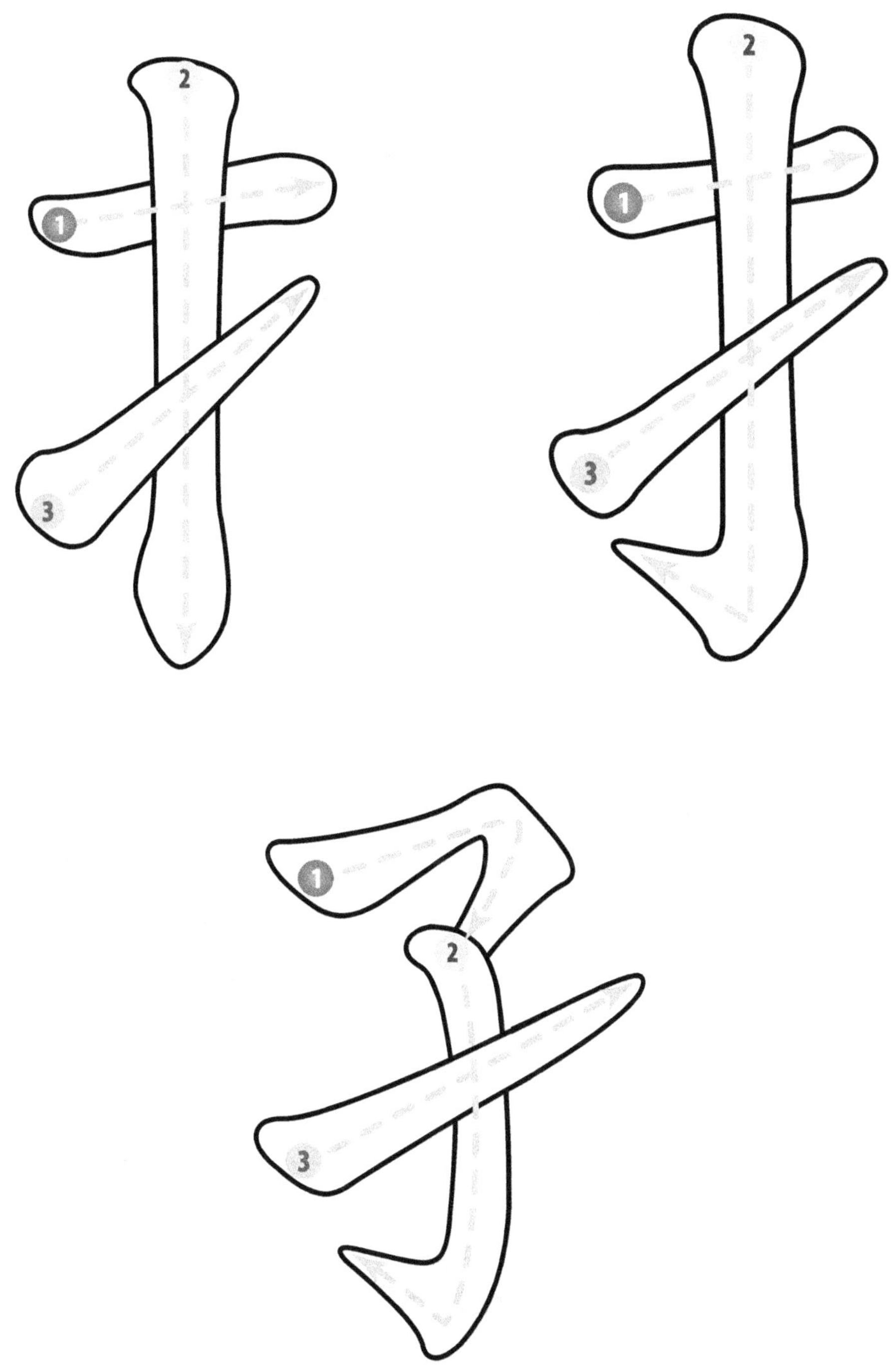

L-Bend Flag

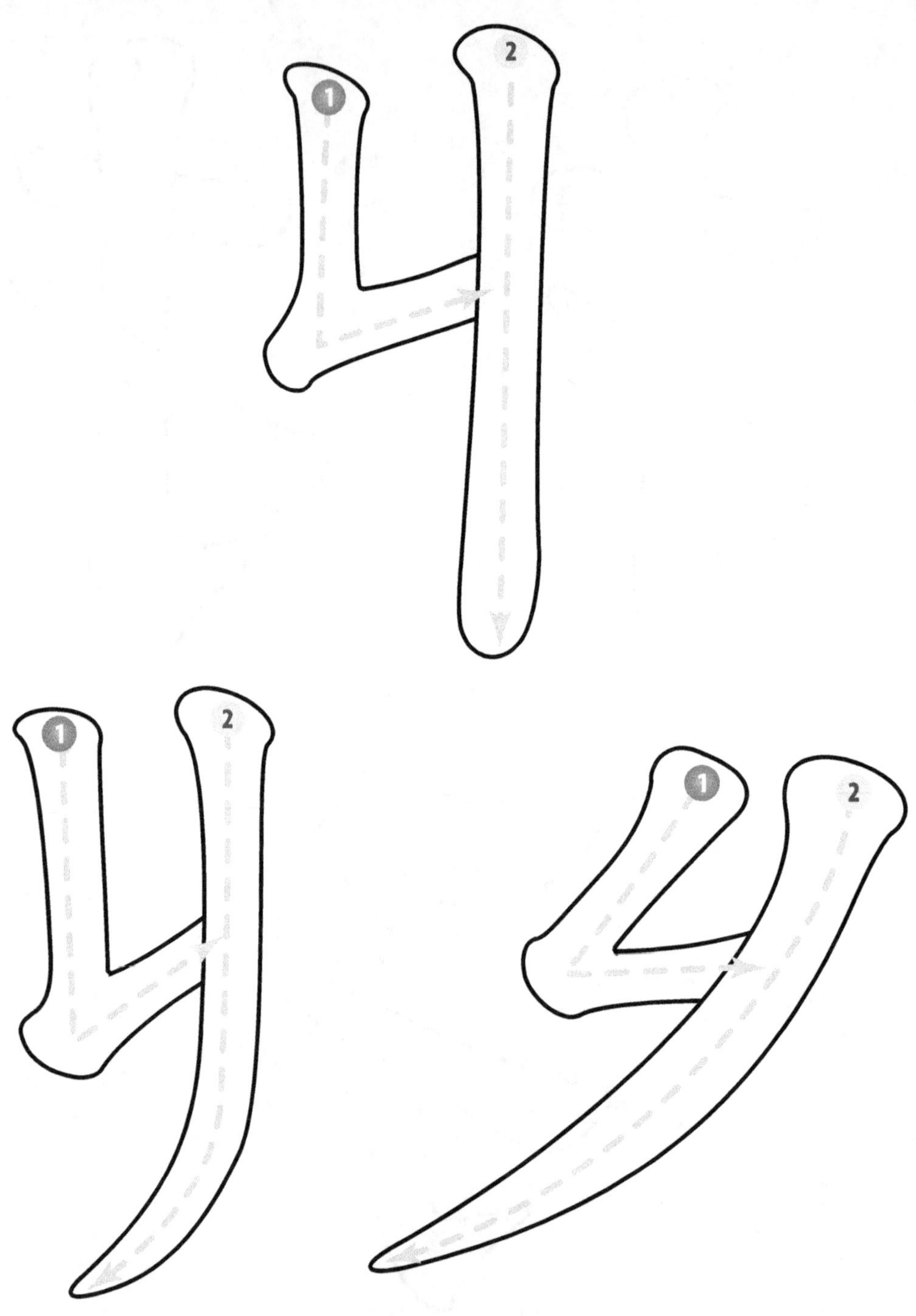

7-Hook Flag

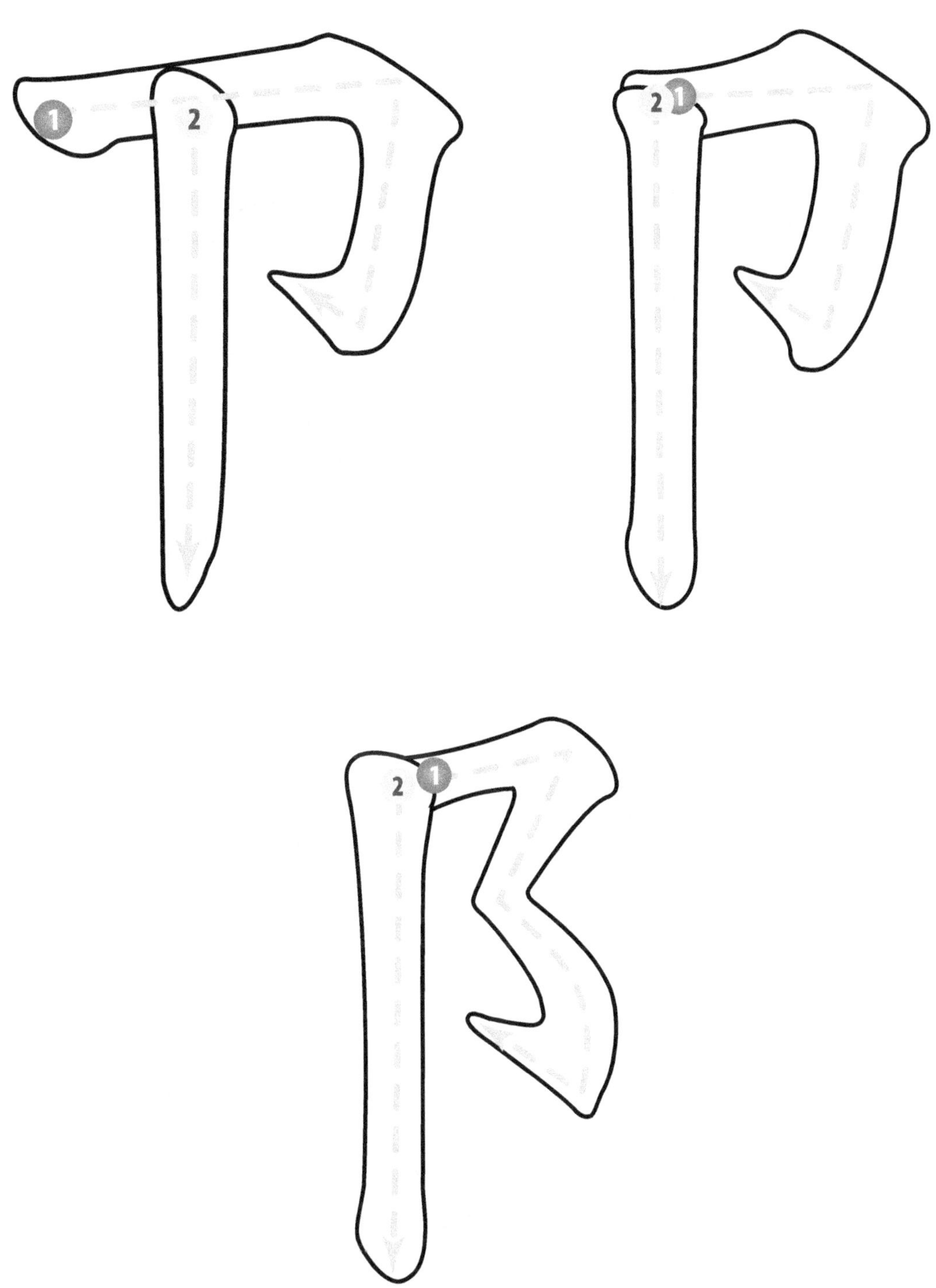

7-Hook Frame

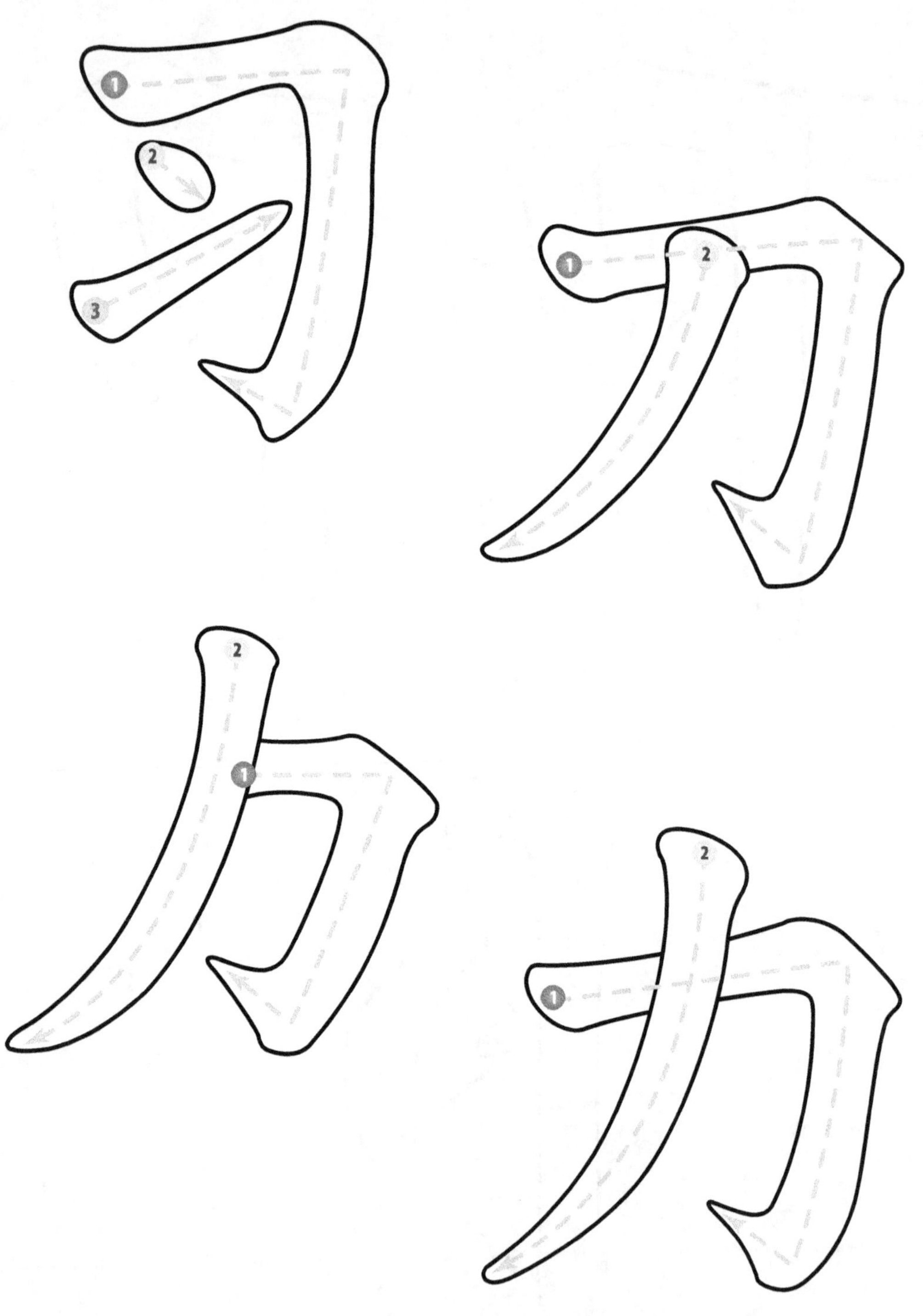

L-Frame & U-Frame

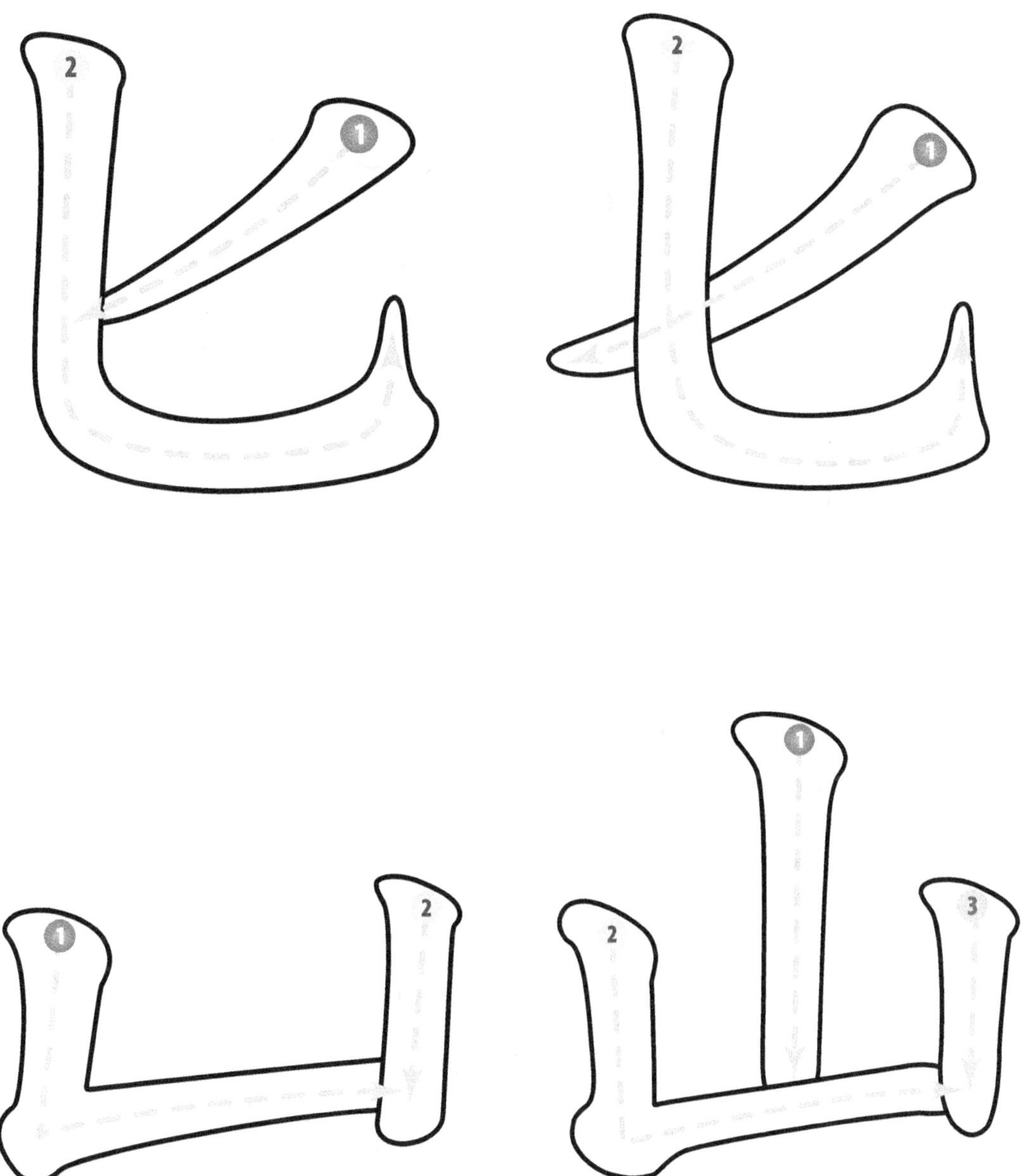

ㄣ-Hook Frame

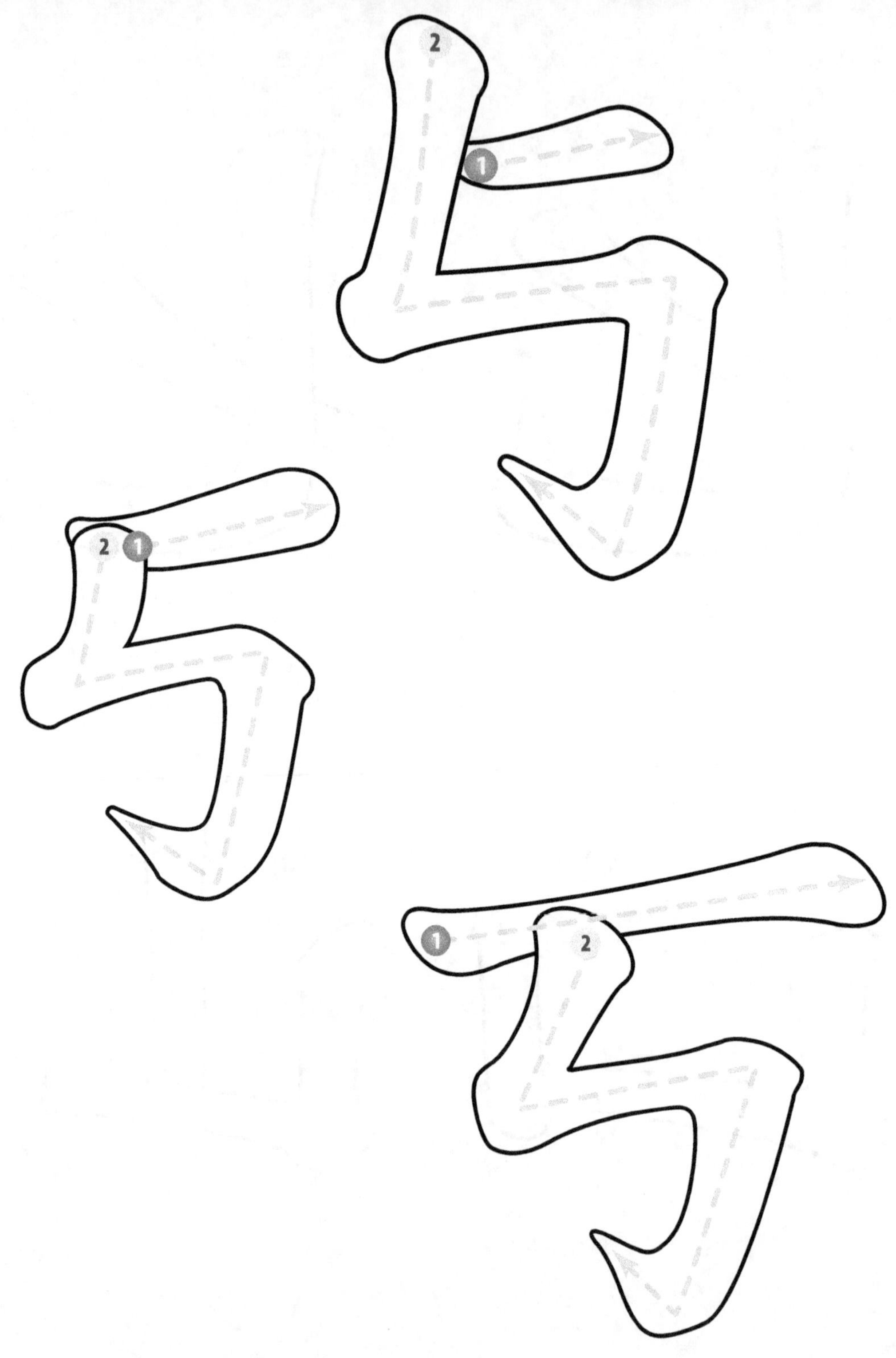

L7-Hook Frame

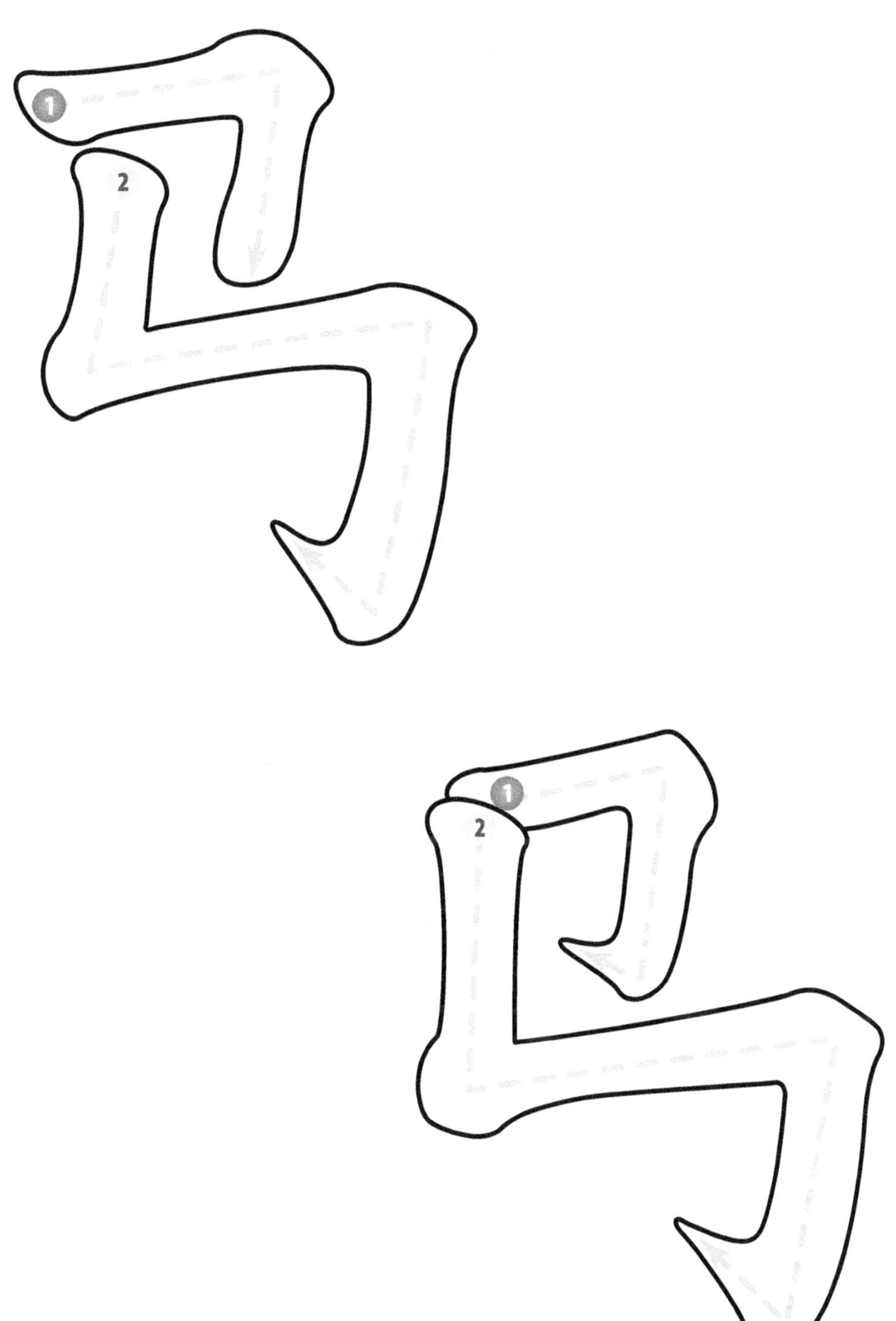

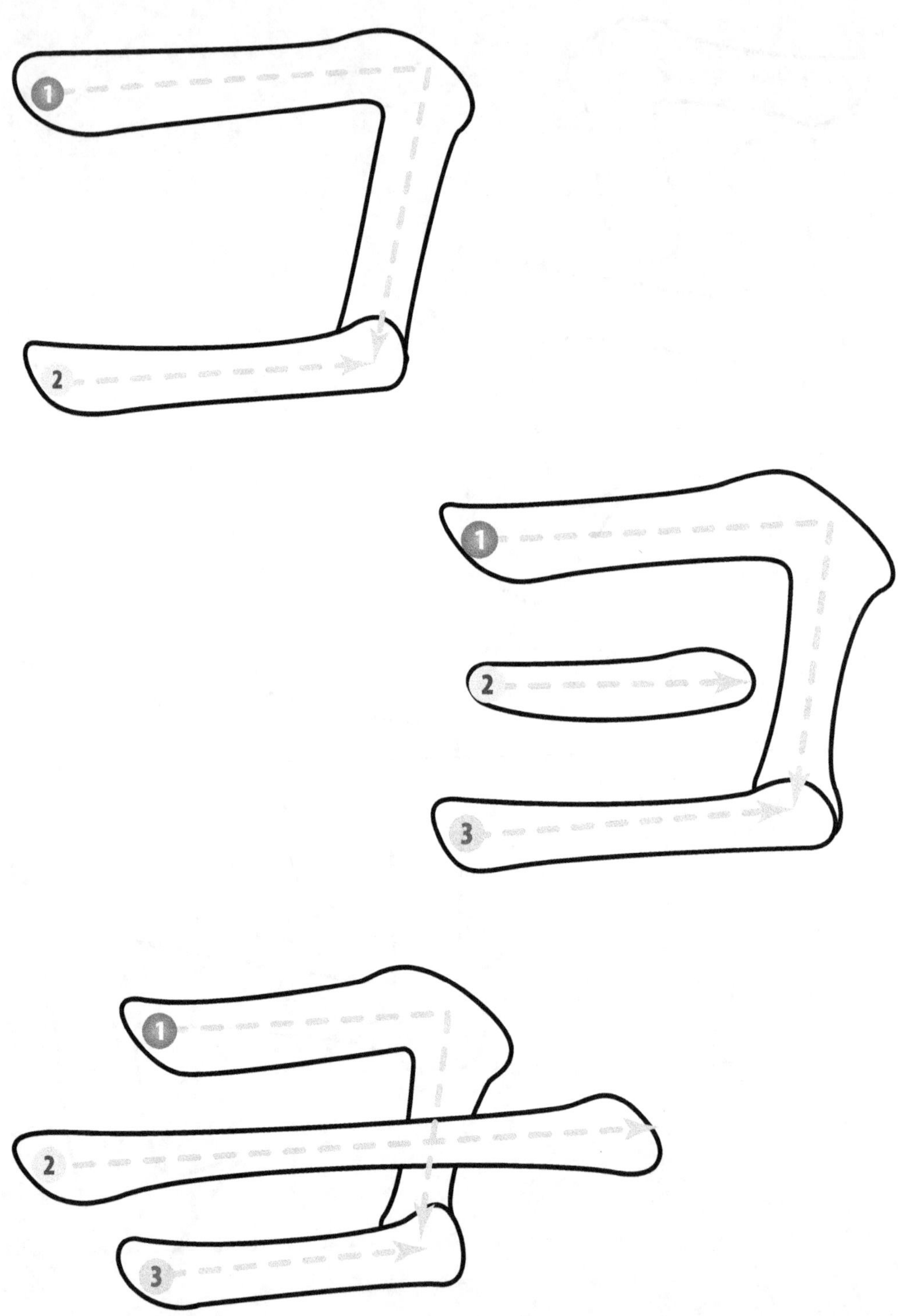

Flipped C

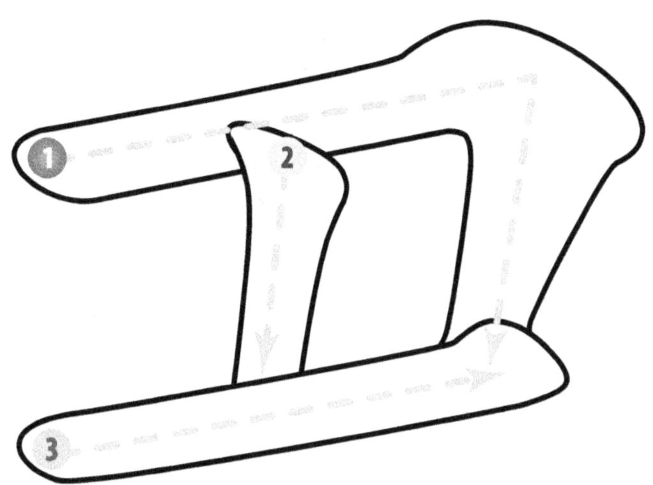

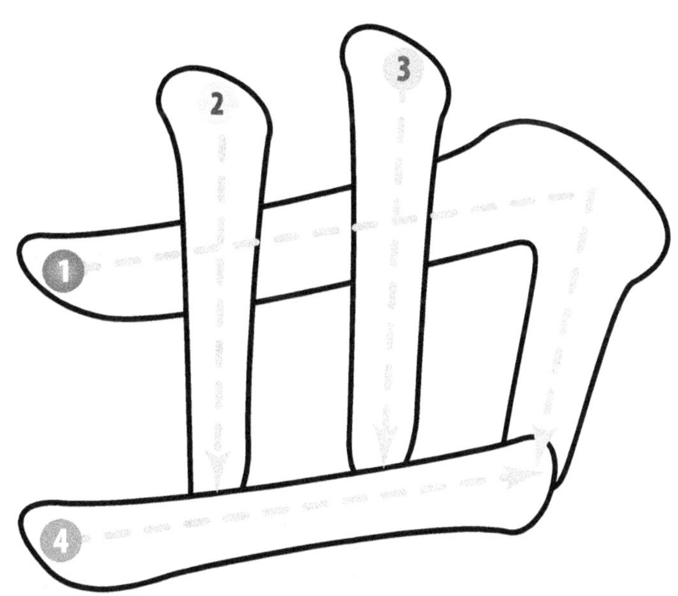

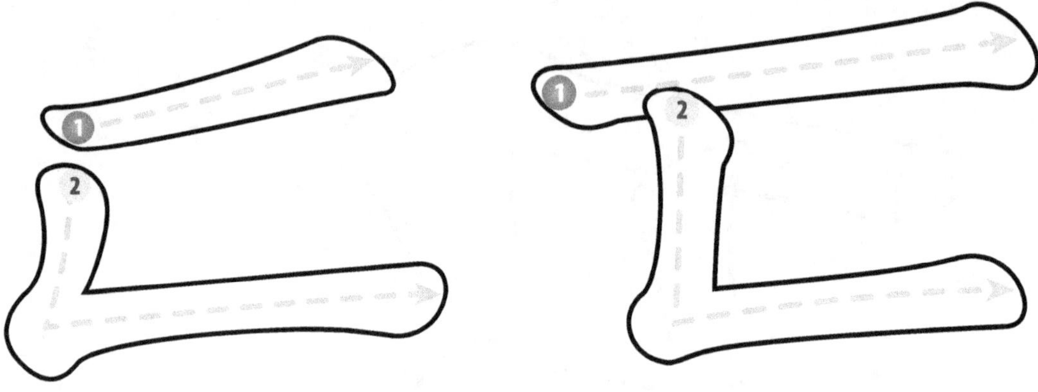

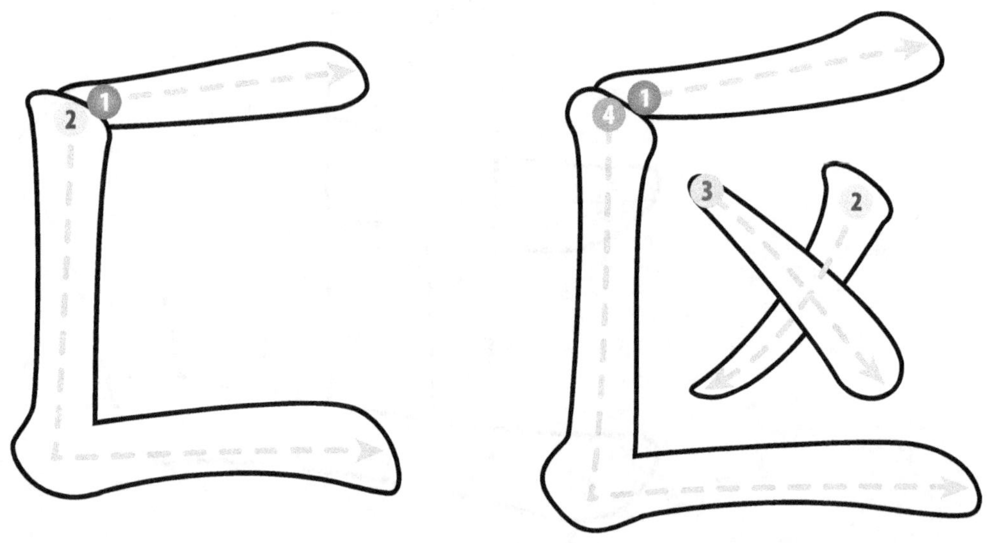

C-Frame

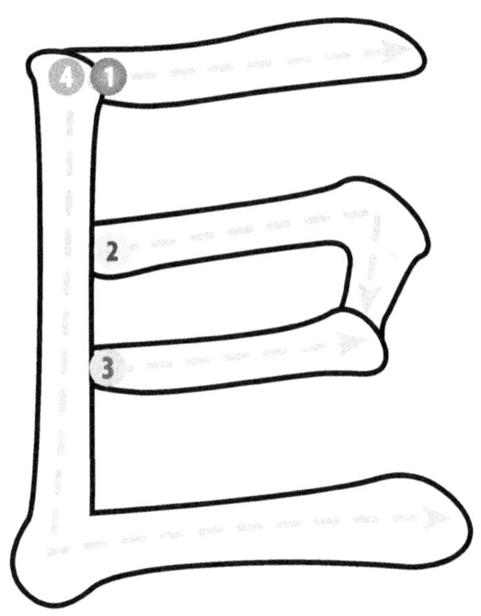

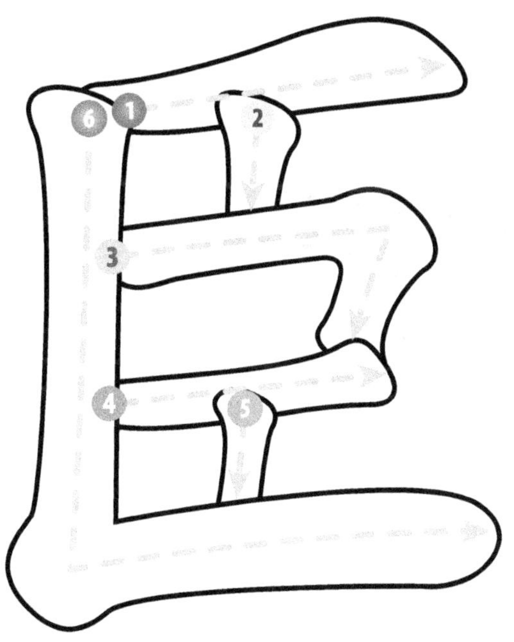

n-Frame

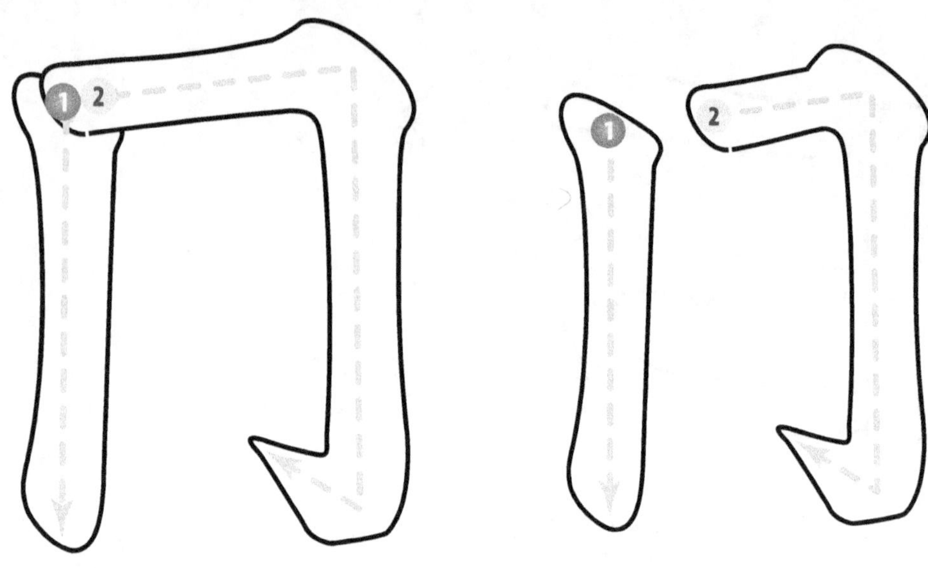

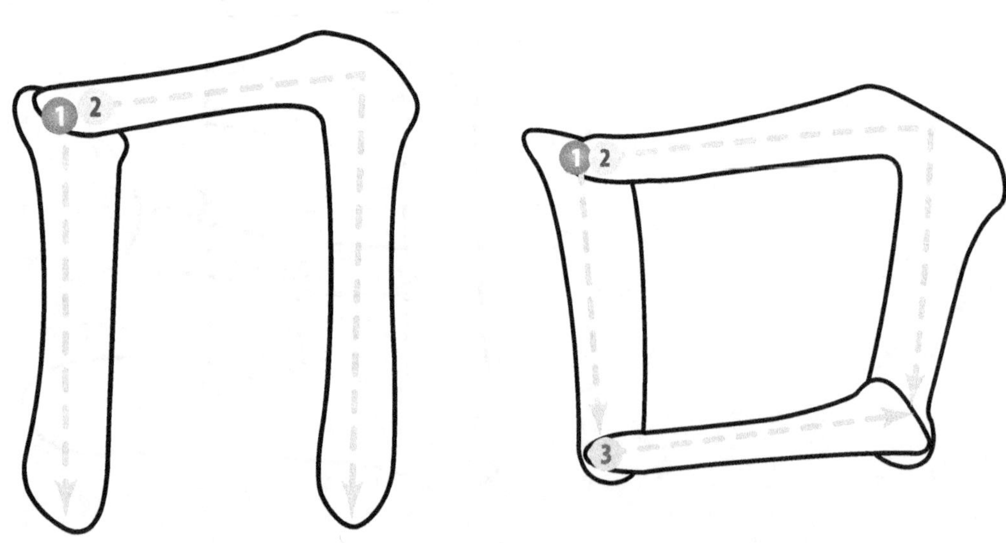

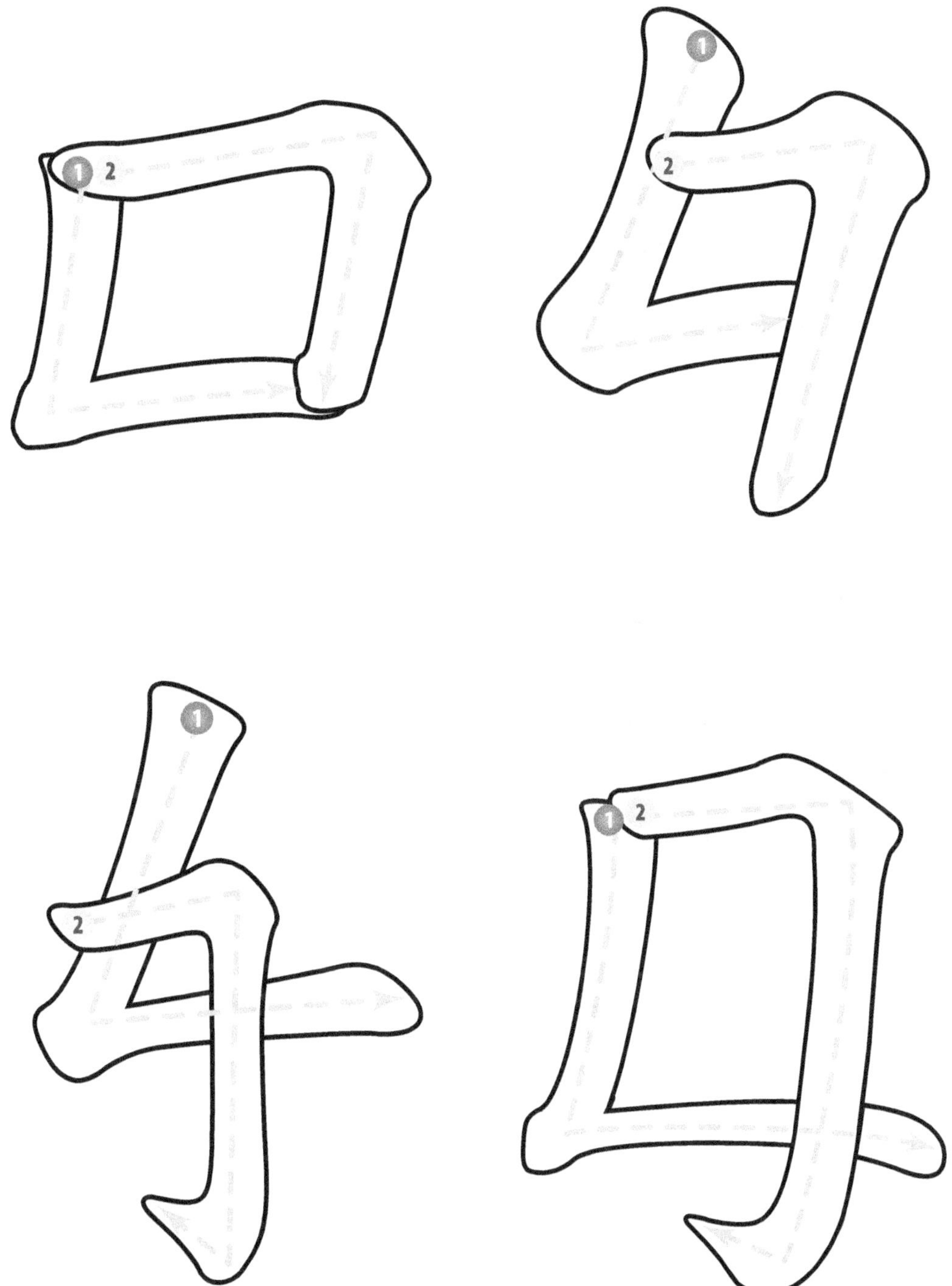

Singe Leg

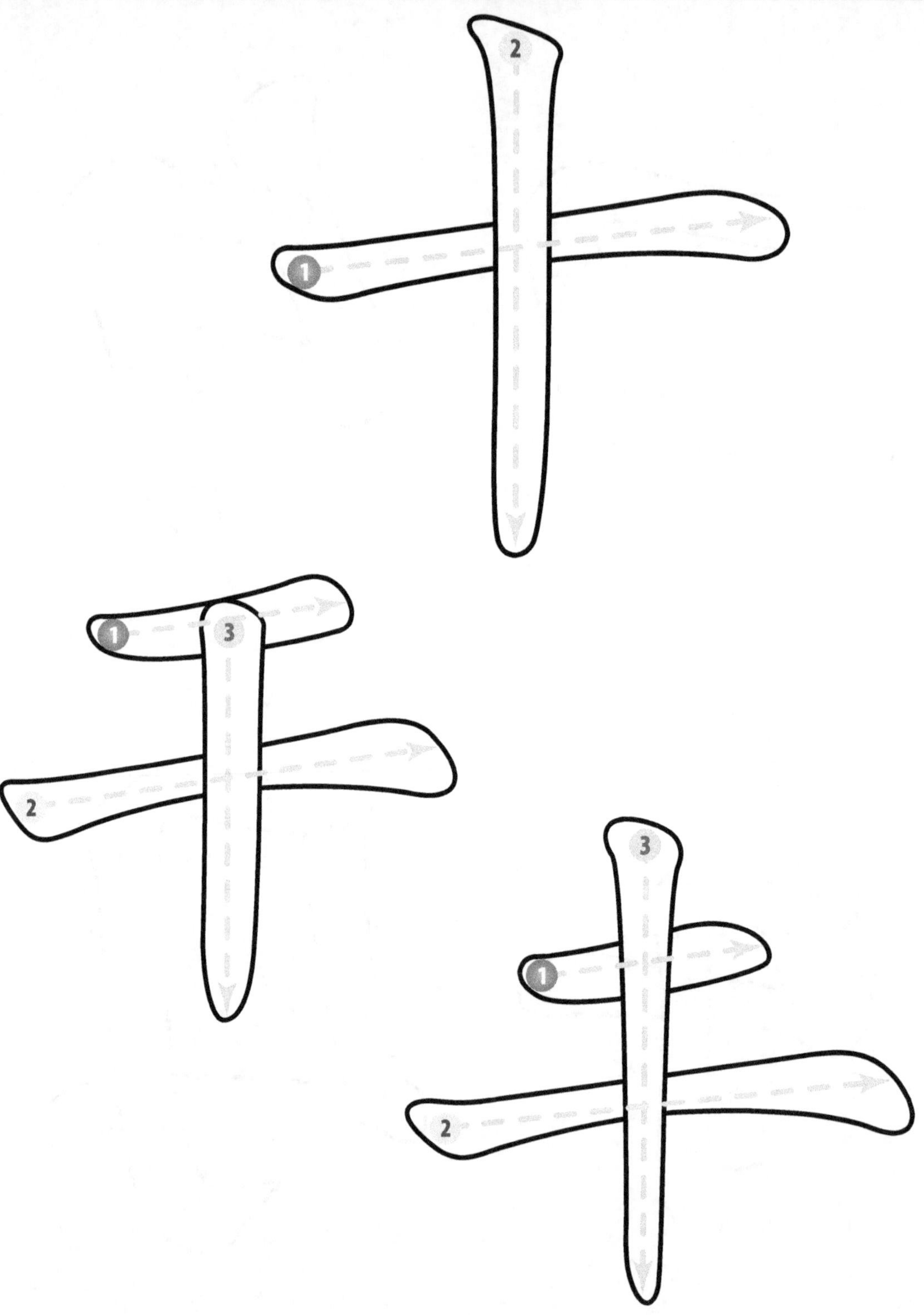

Single Leg

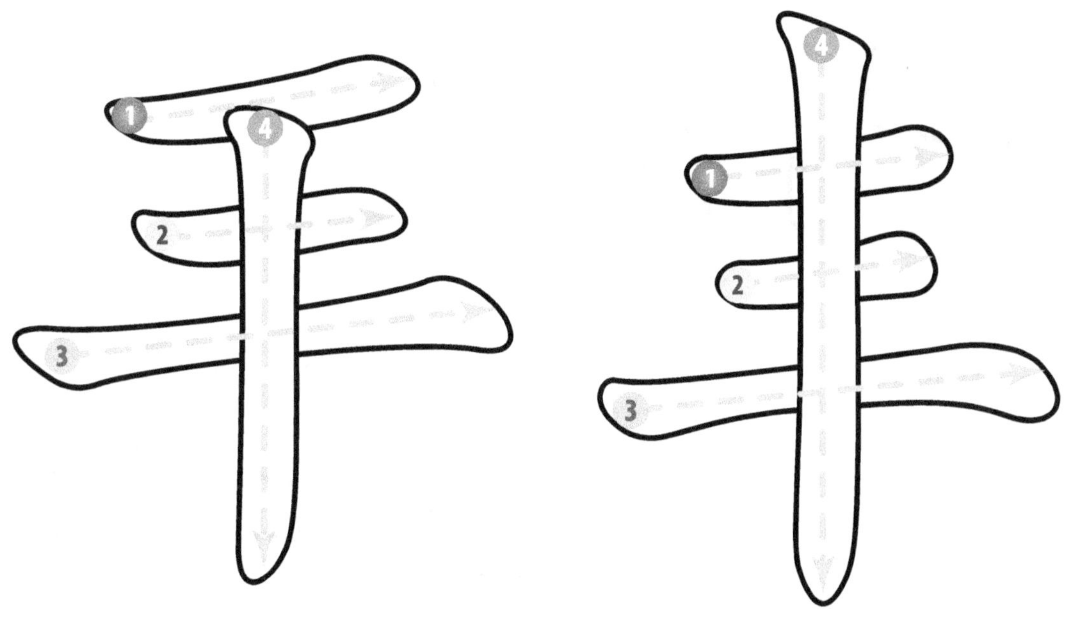

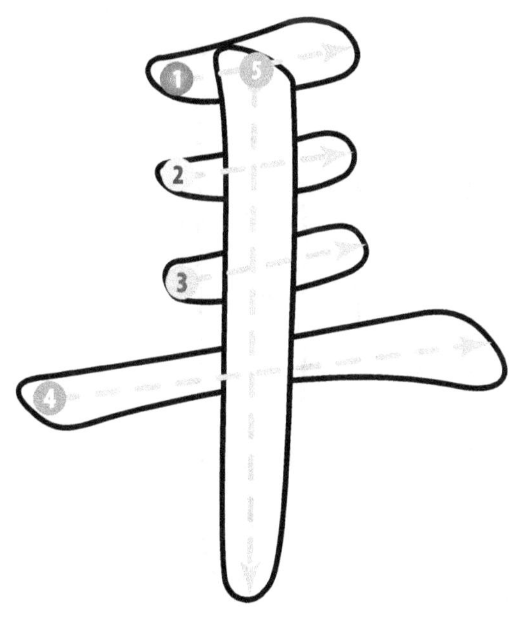

Multiple Legs

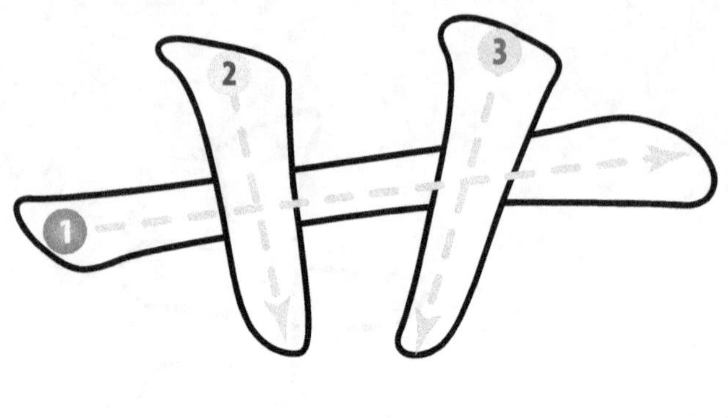

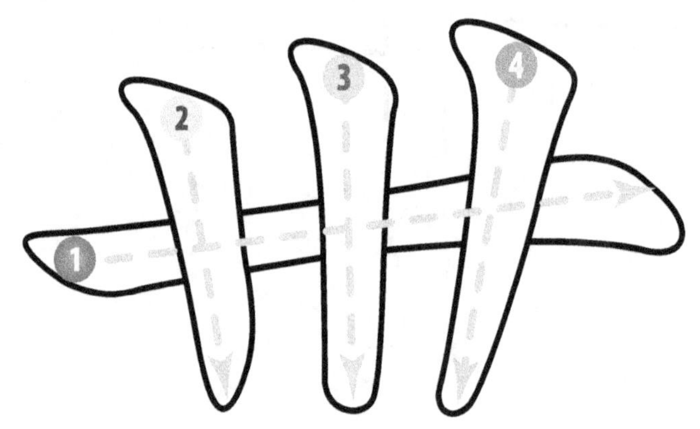

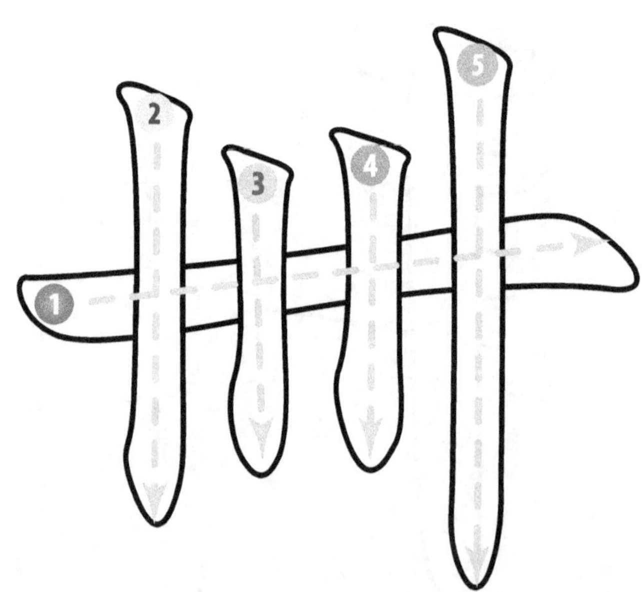

Multiple Legs

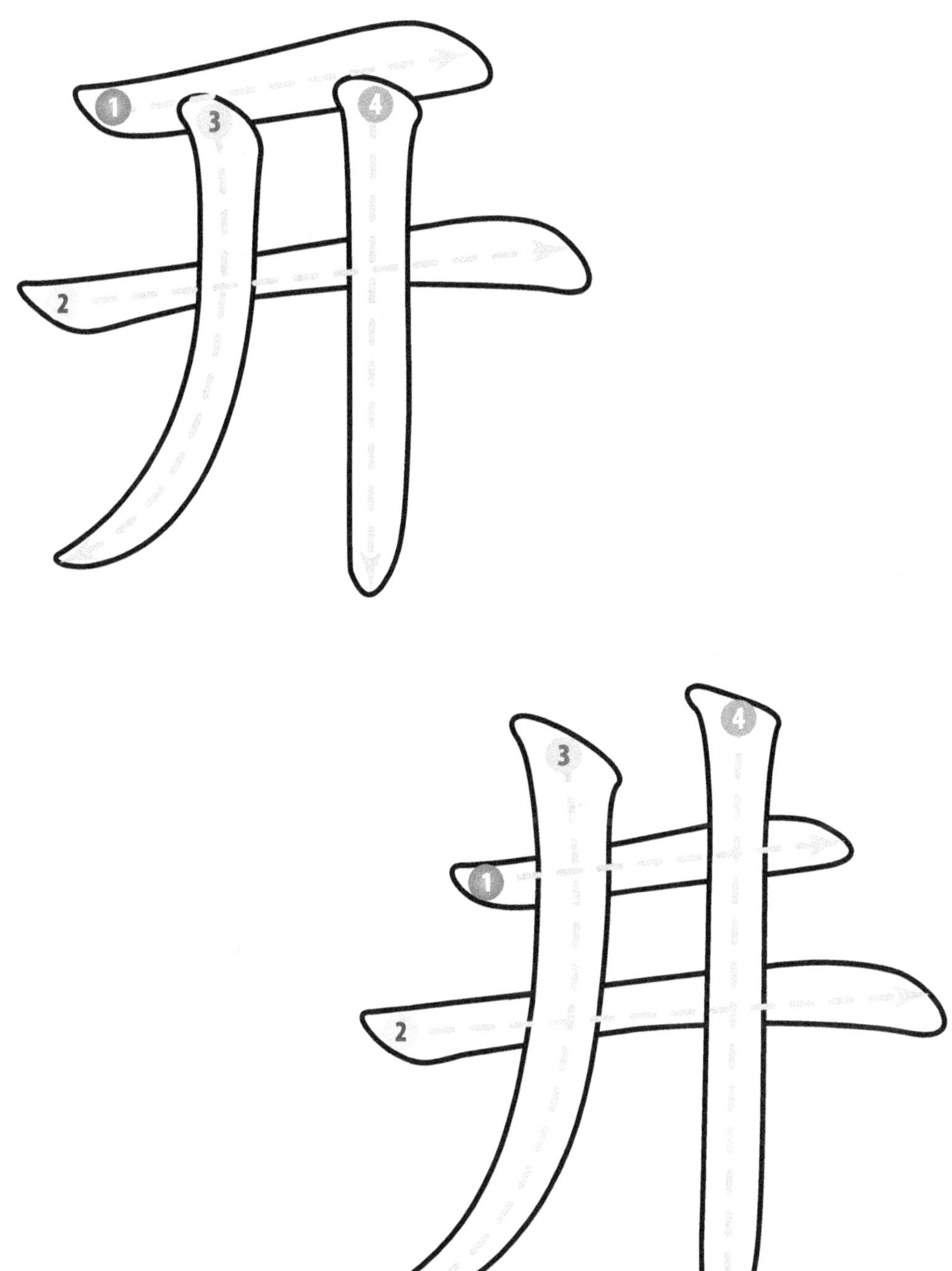

Split Intersections

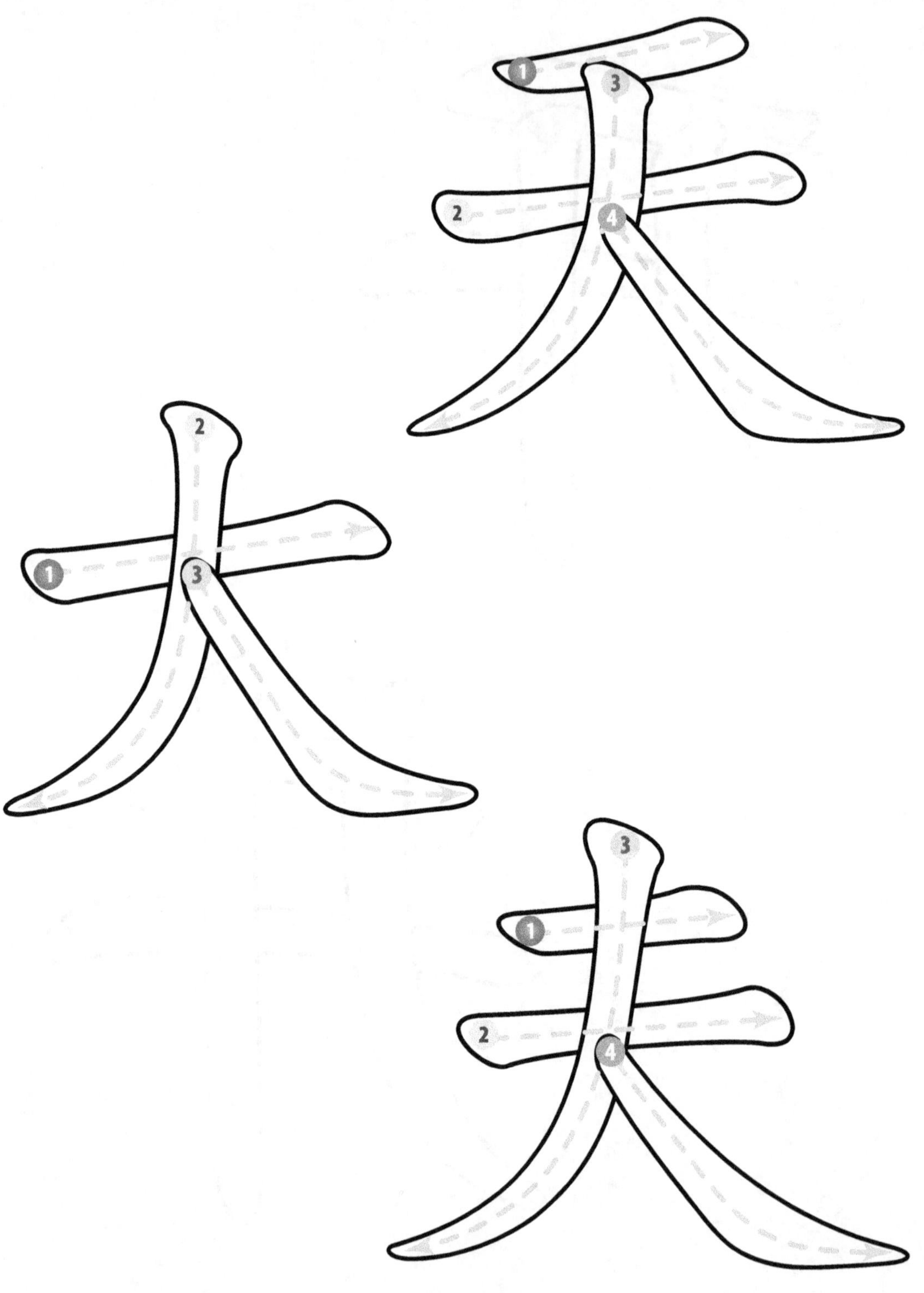

Split Intersections

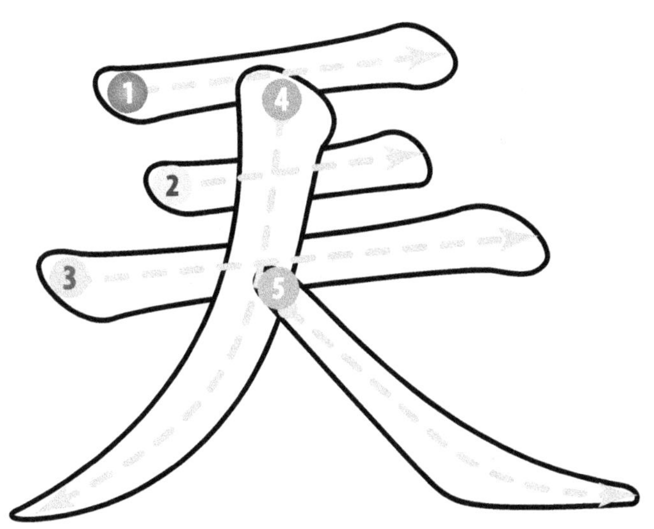

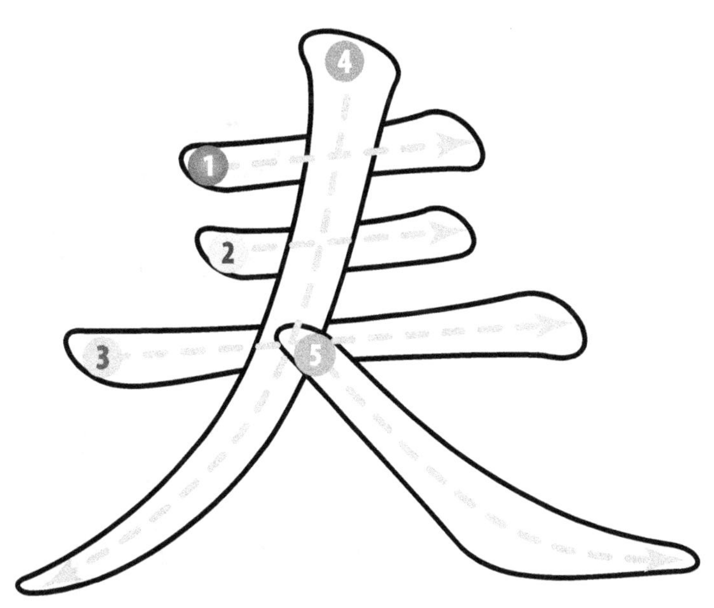

Tripod

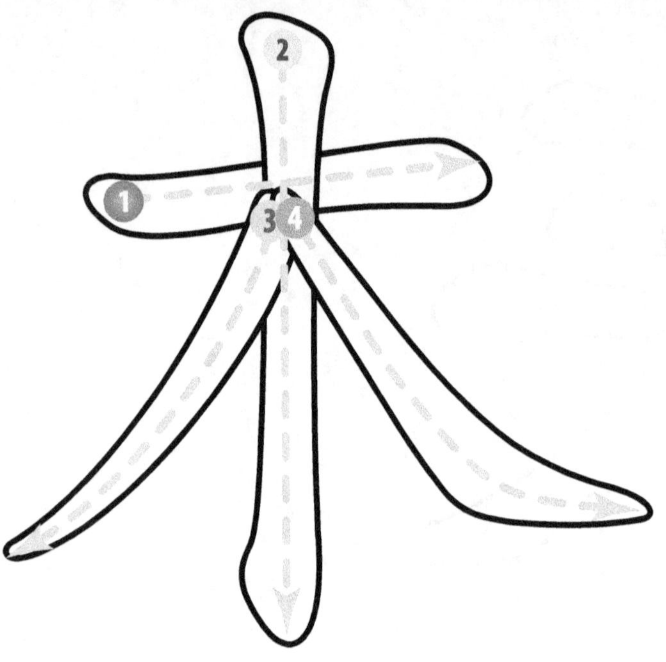

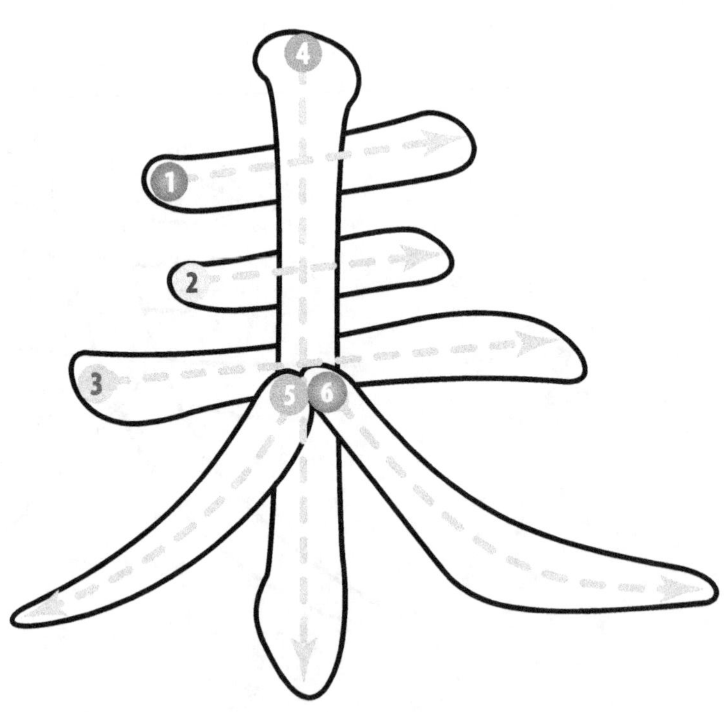

Tripod

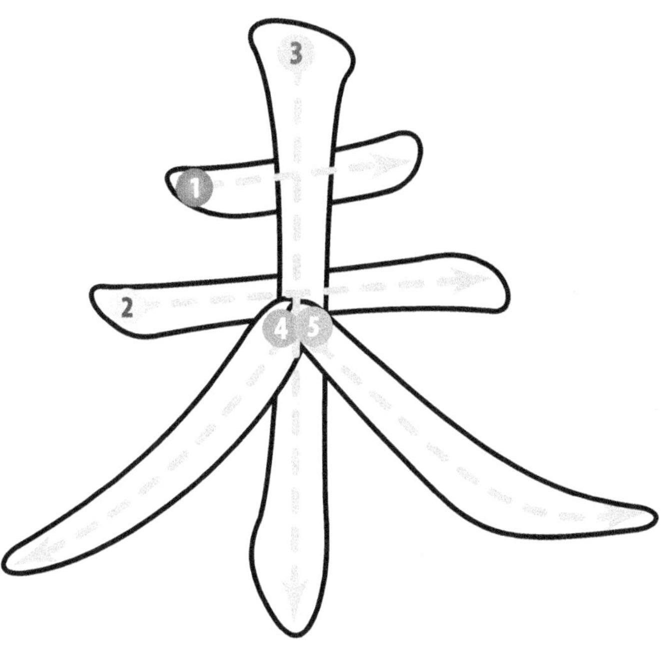

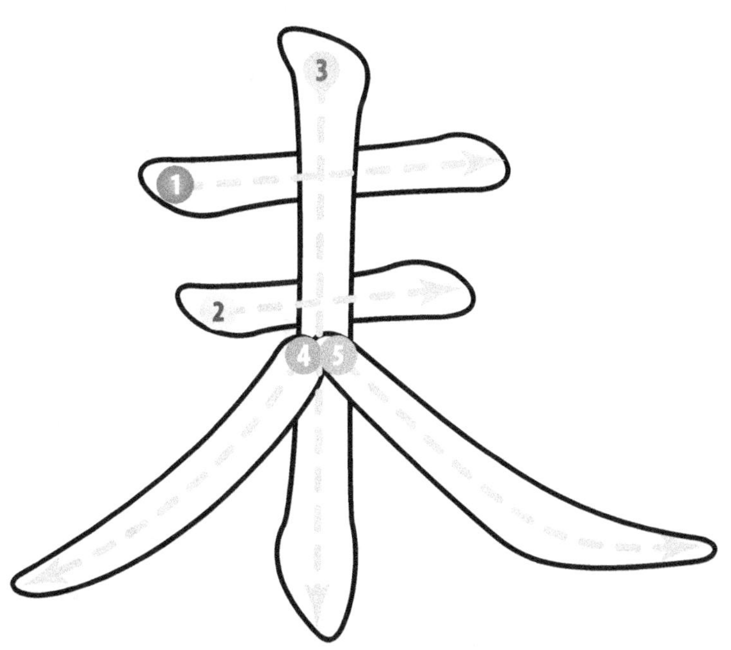

Intersections (Flat)

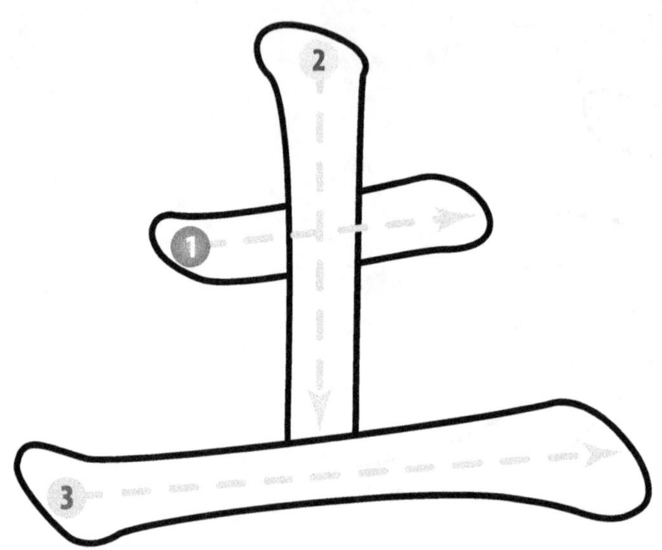

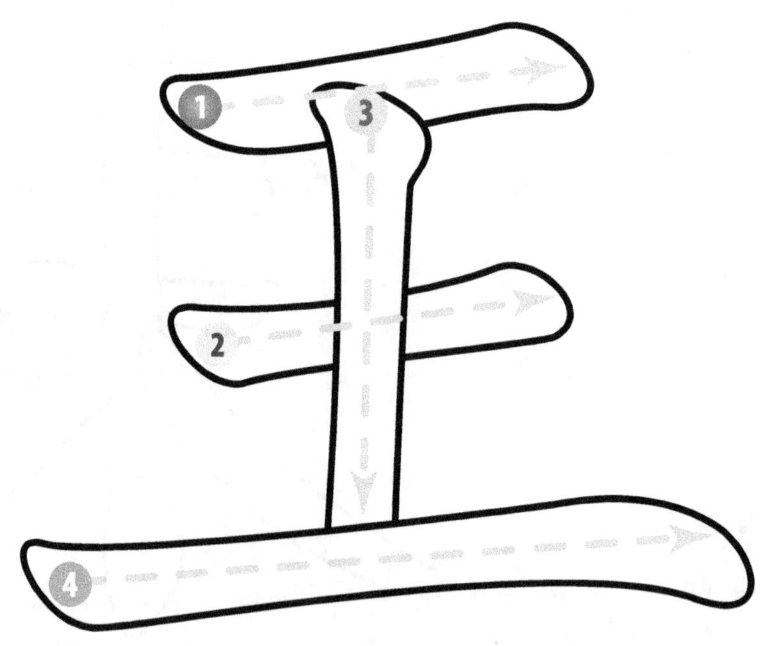

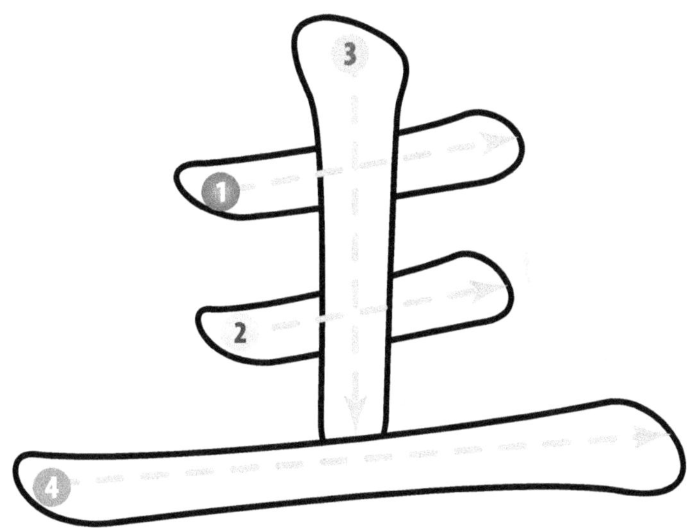

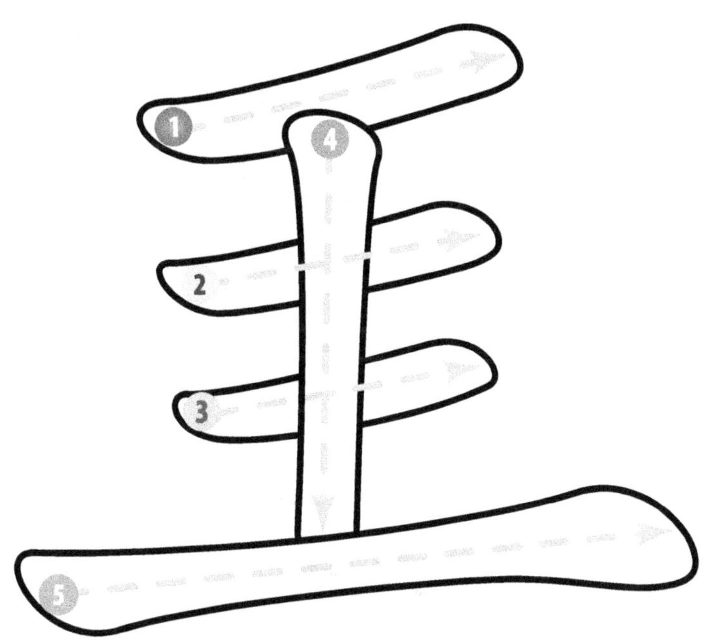

Intersections (Flat)

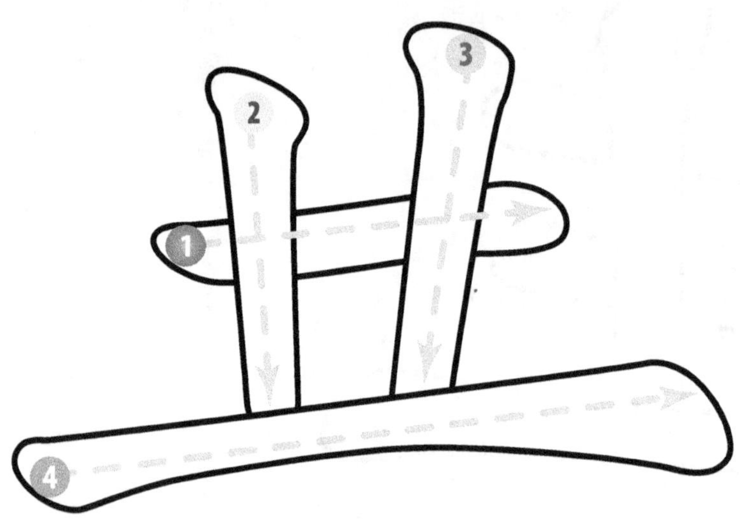

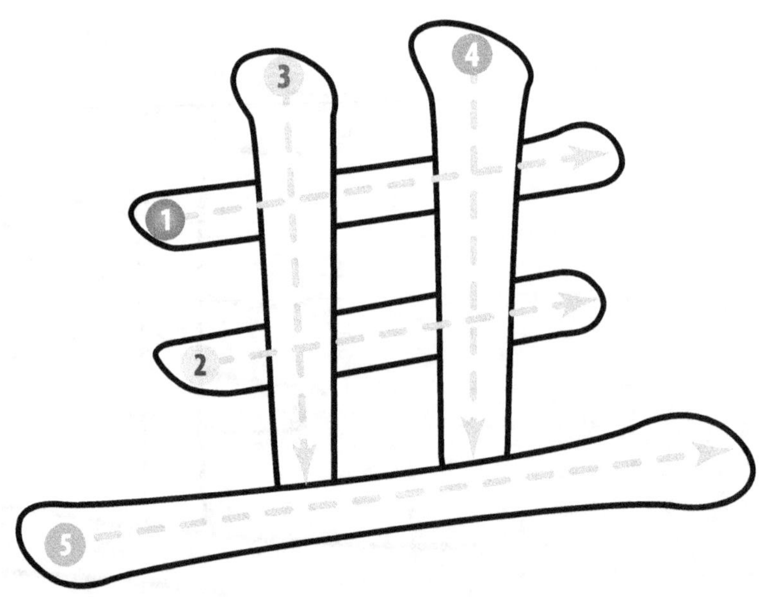

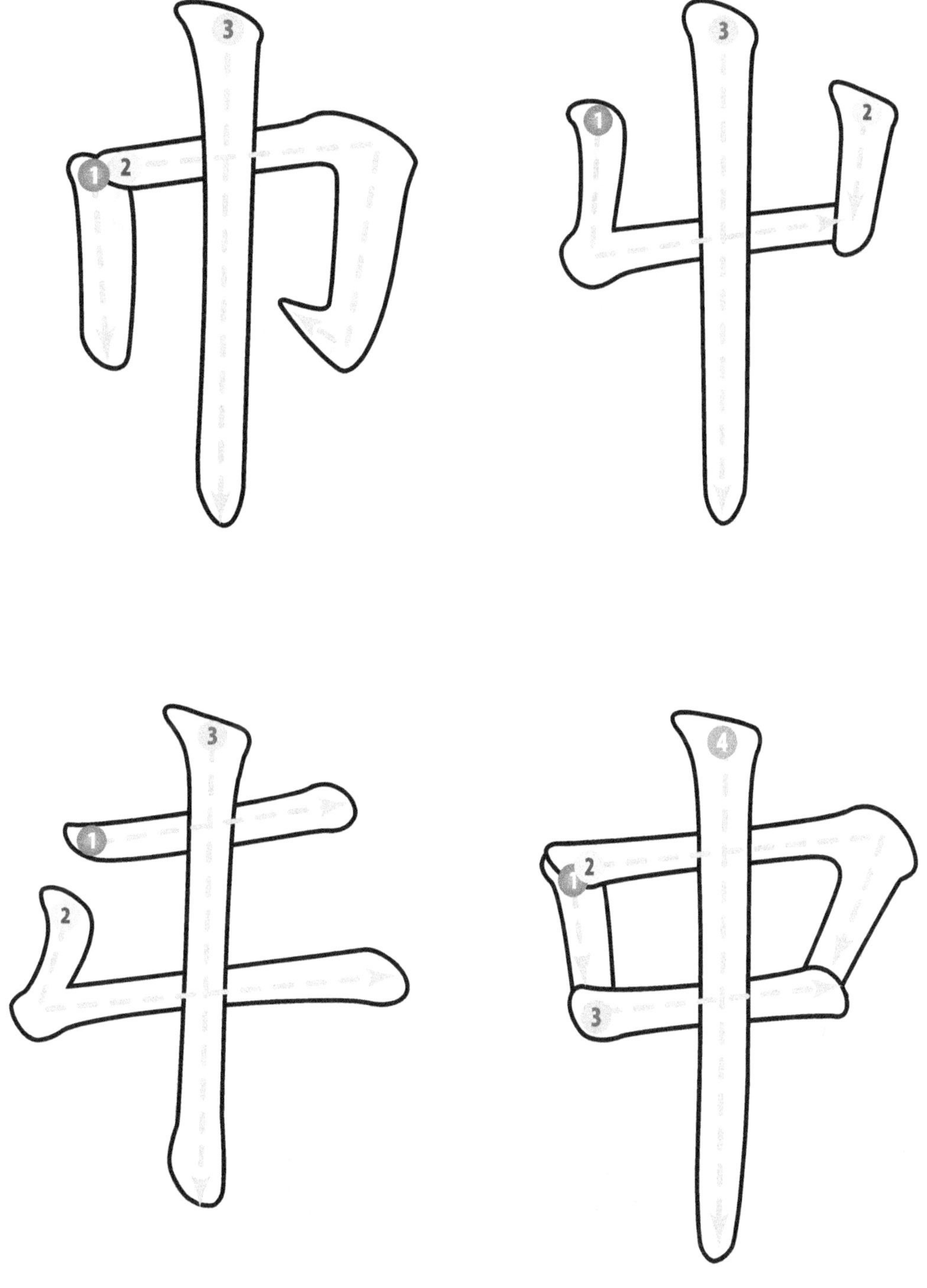

Horizontals Enclosure

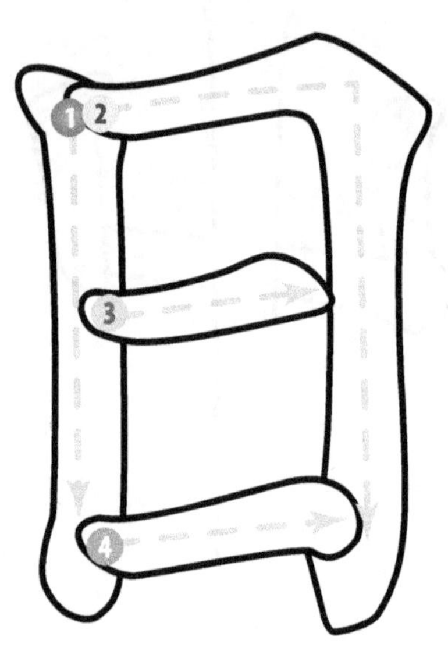

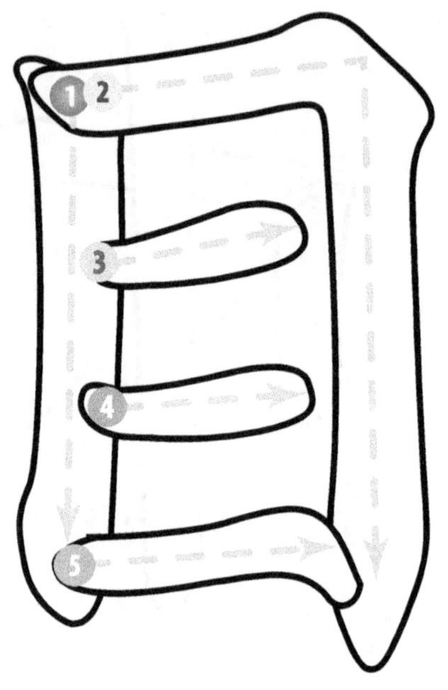

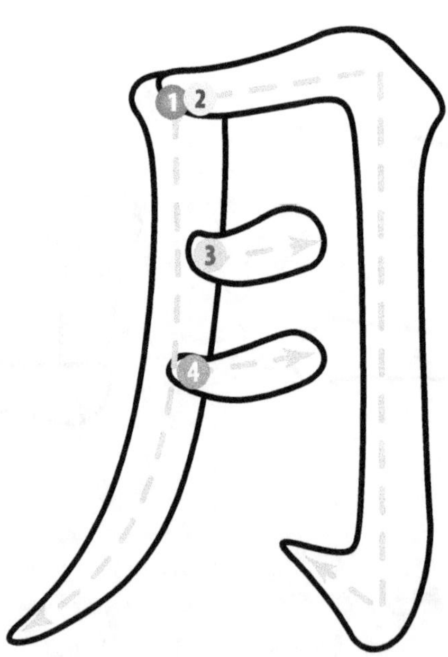

Horizontals Enclosure

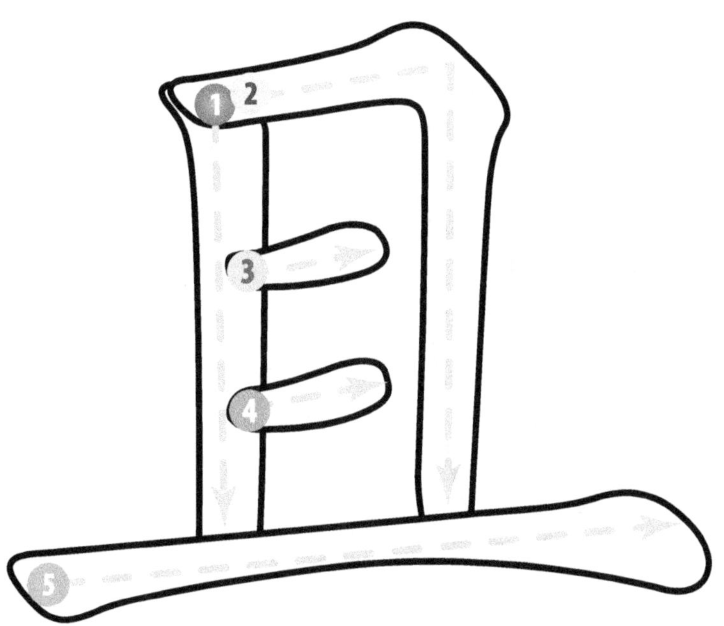

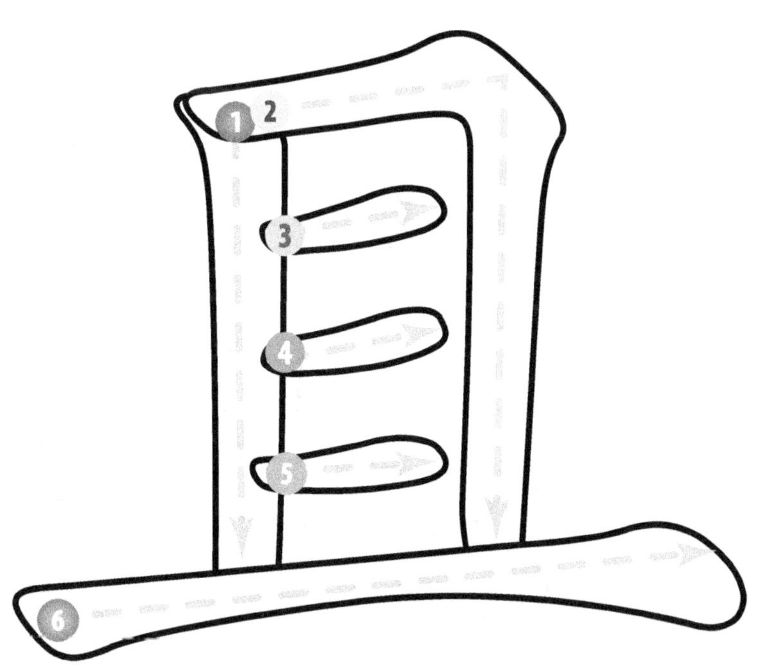

Verticals Enclosure

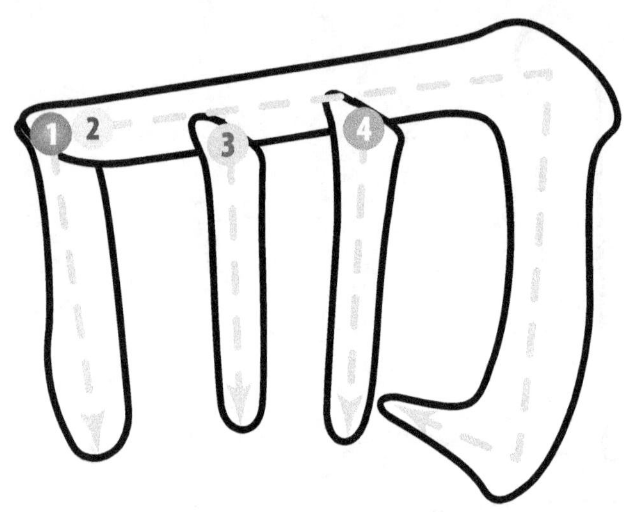

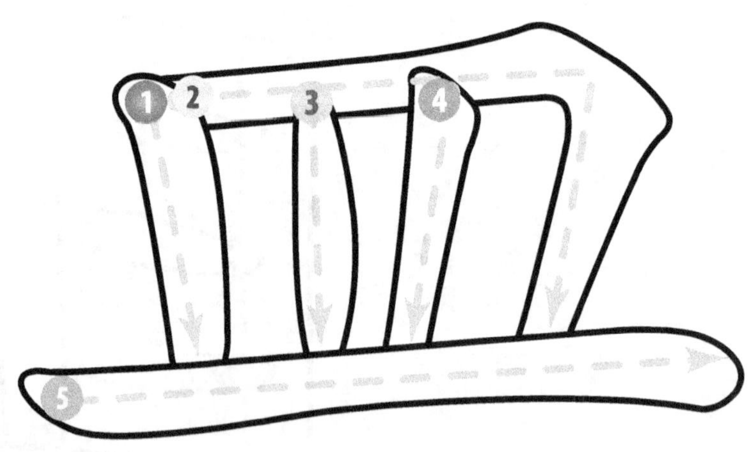

Verticals Enclosure

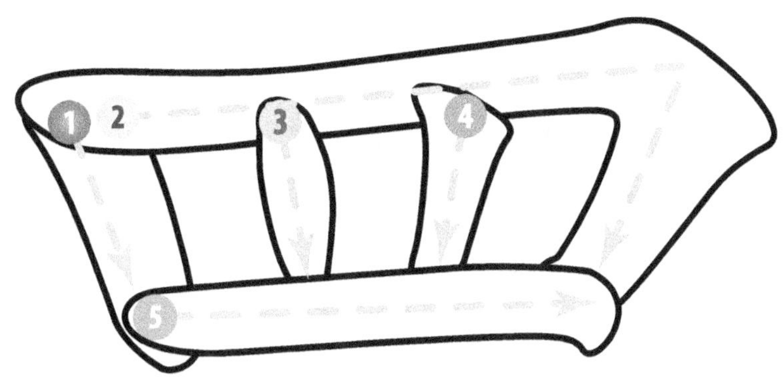

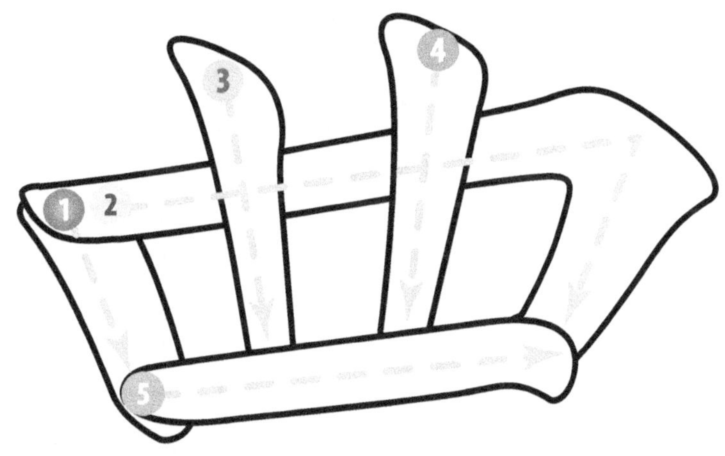

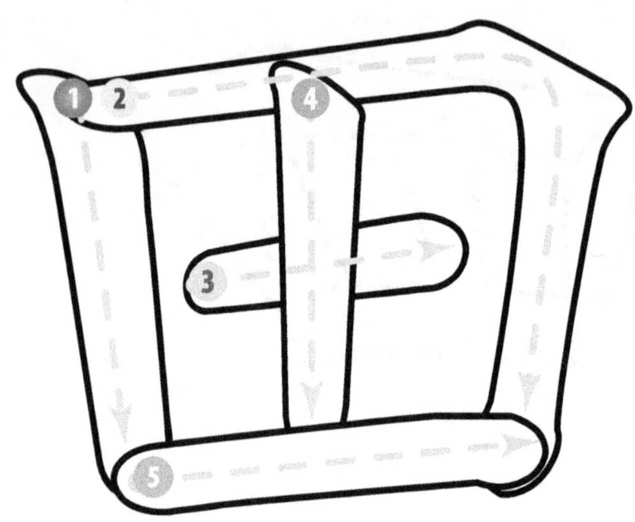

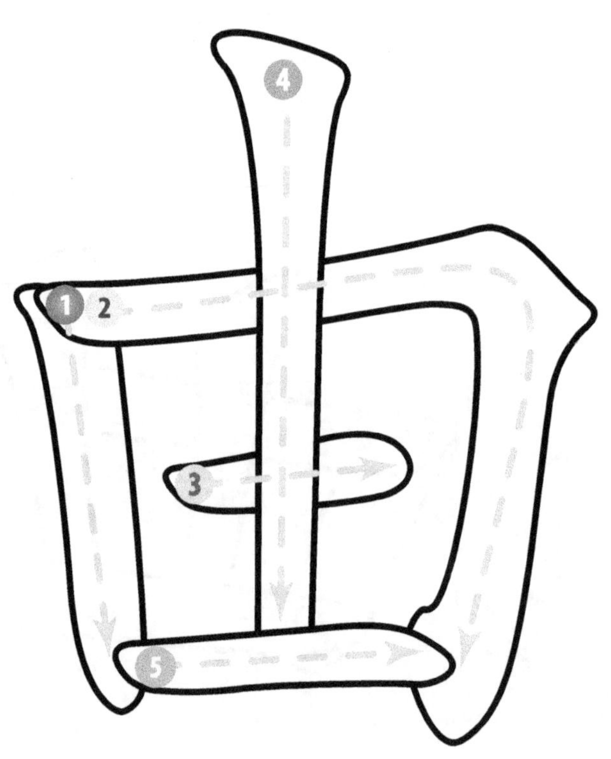

Intersections Enclosure

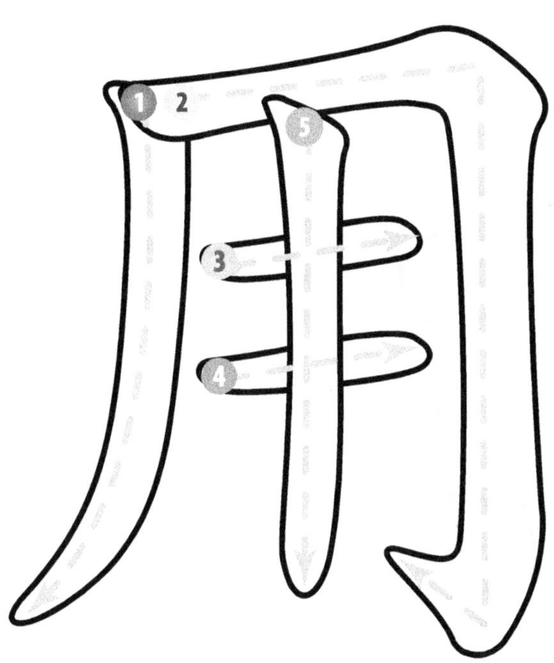

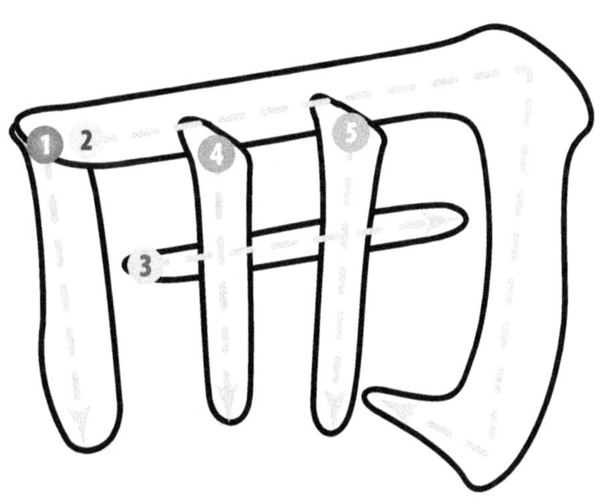

Enclosure (Intersections)

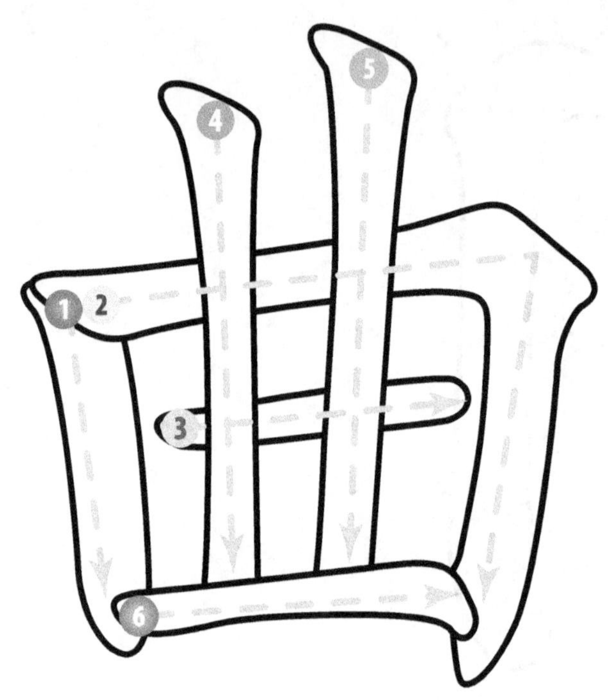

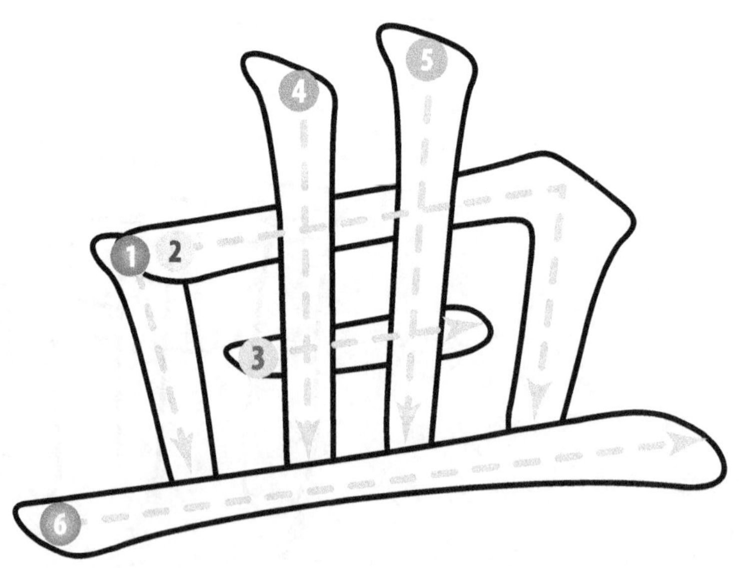

Parallels

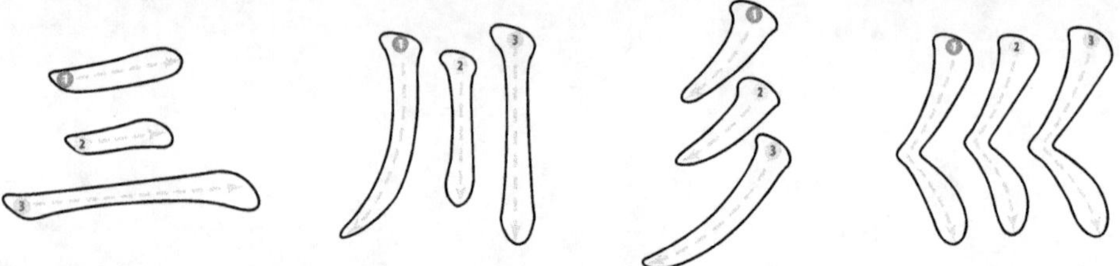

Dots (Left to Right)

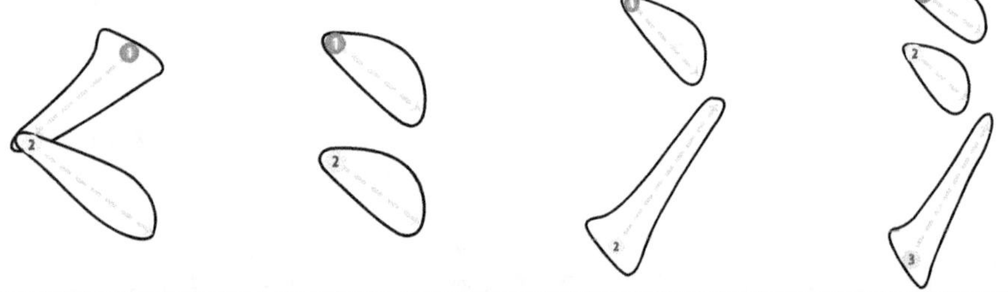

Dots (Top to Bottom)

Final Dot

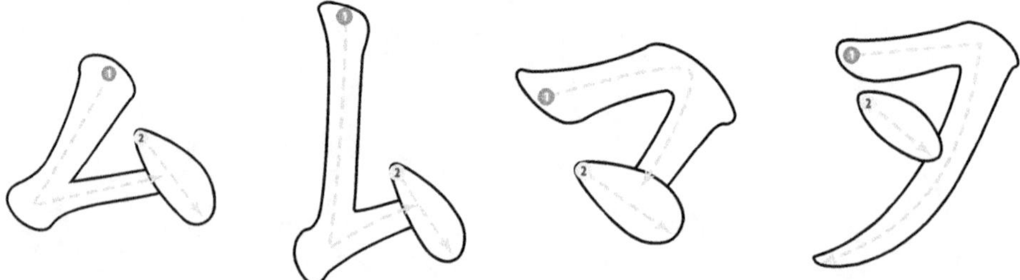

T-Shape

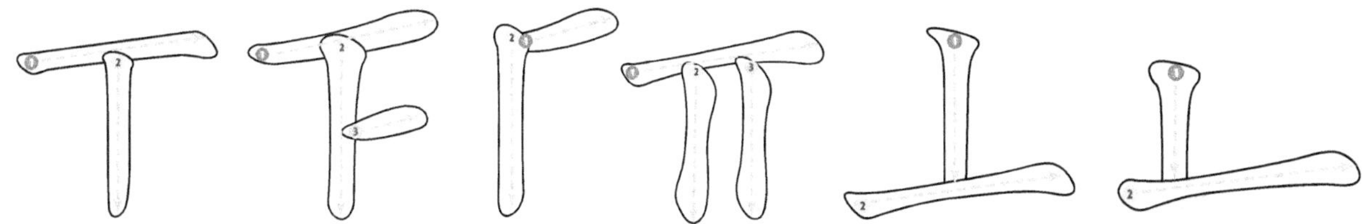

Half Ladder

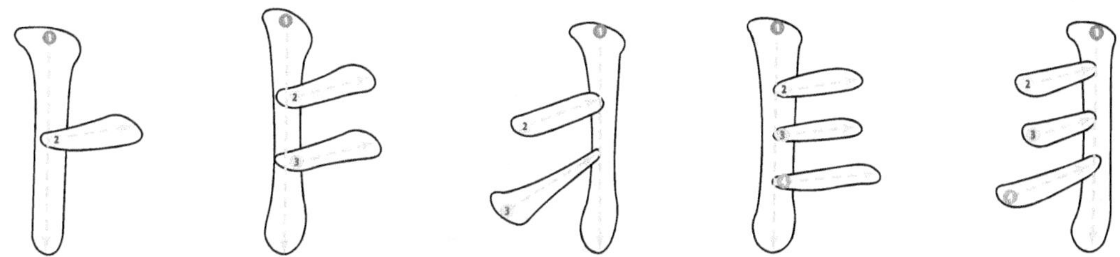

Split

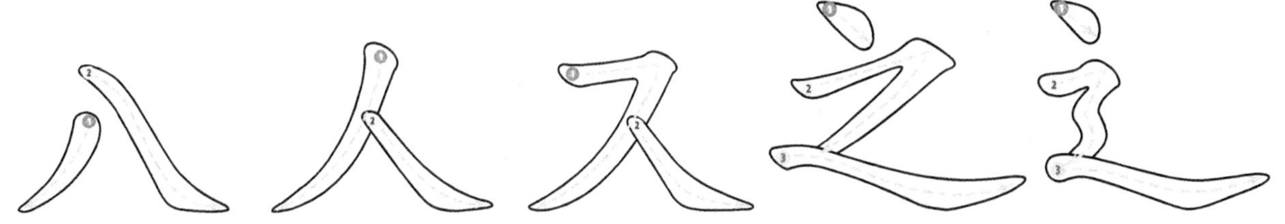

Vertical Split / Horizontal Split

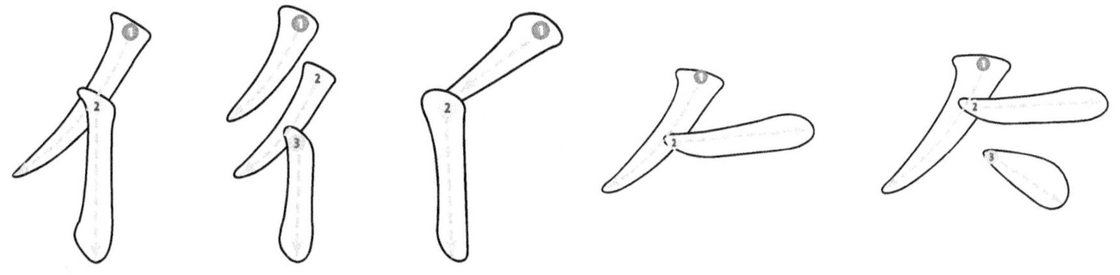

Slide

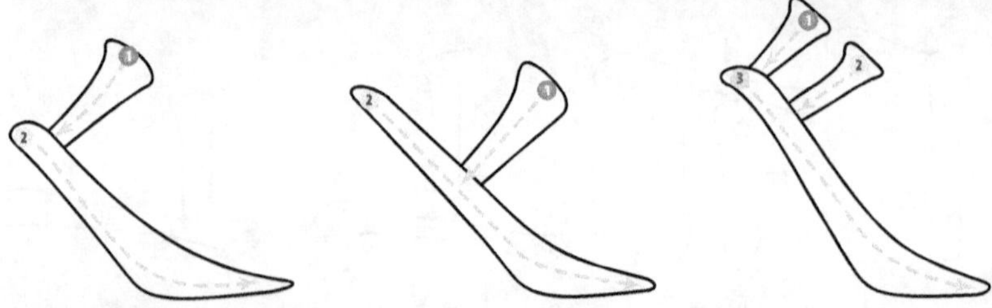

7-Slash Split

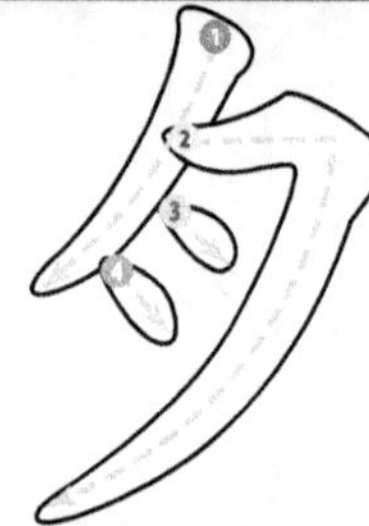

7L-Hook Split

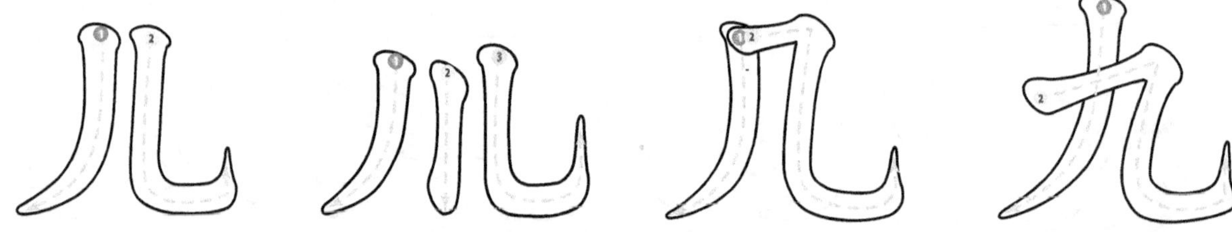

Cross

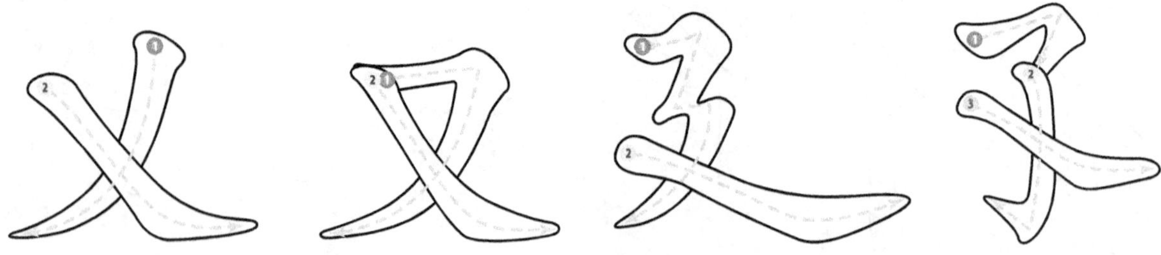

Marching

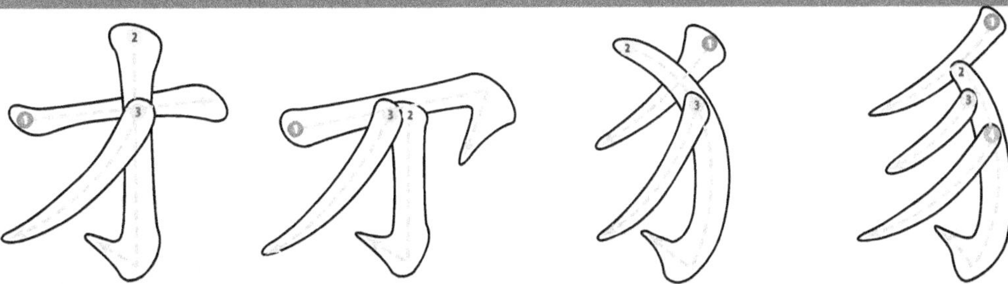

Tick

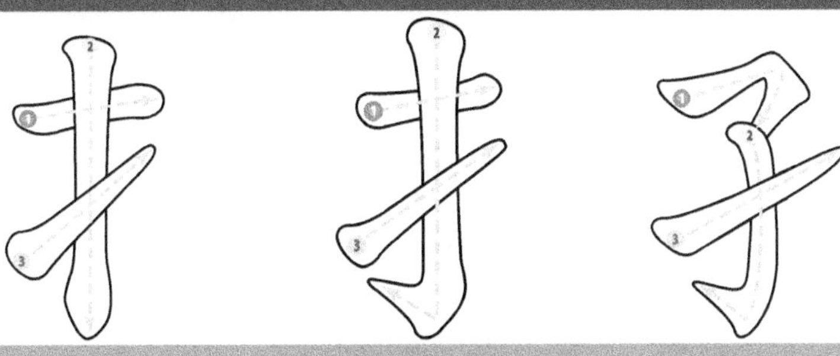

L-Bend Flag

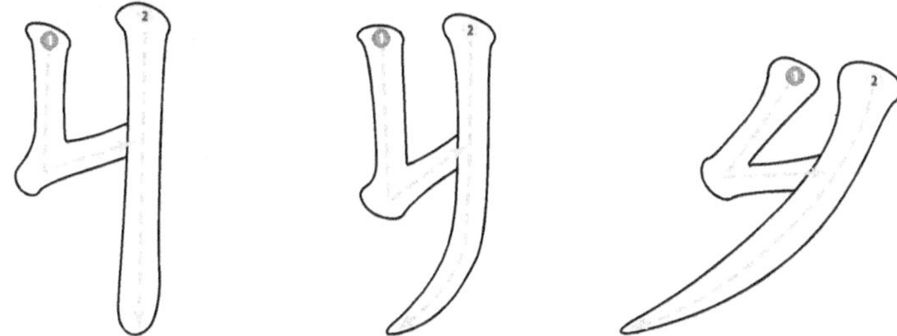

7-Hook Flag

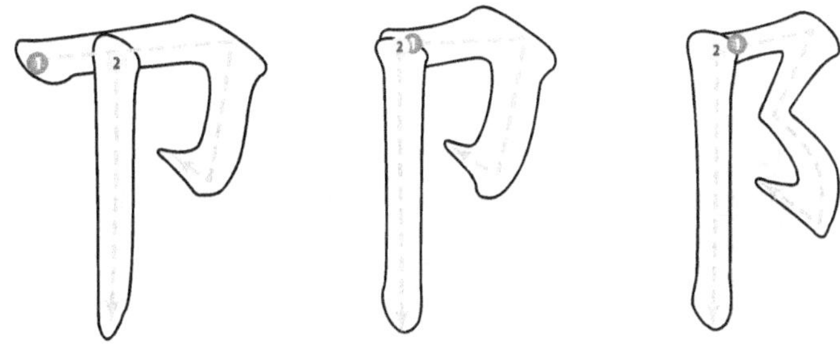

7-Hook Frame

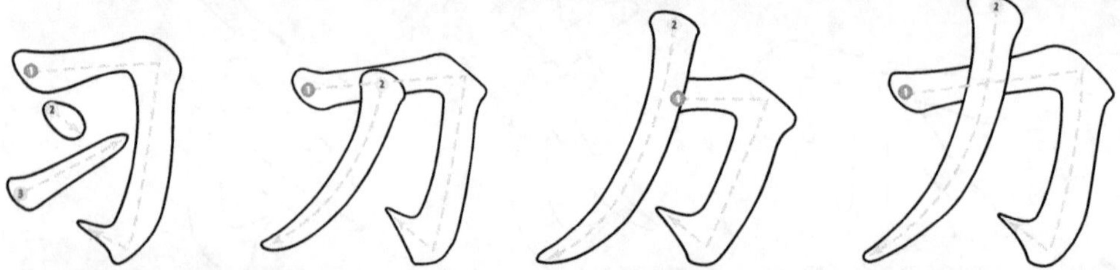

L-Frame n U-Frame

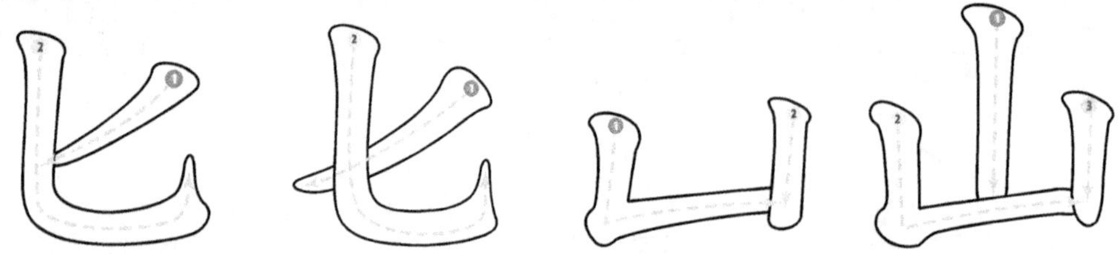

L7-Hook Frame

Flipped C

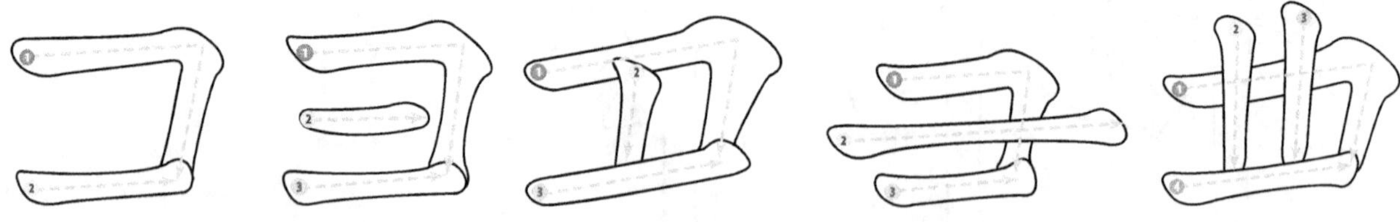

C-Frame

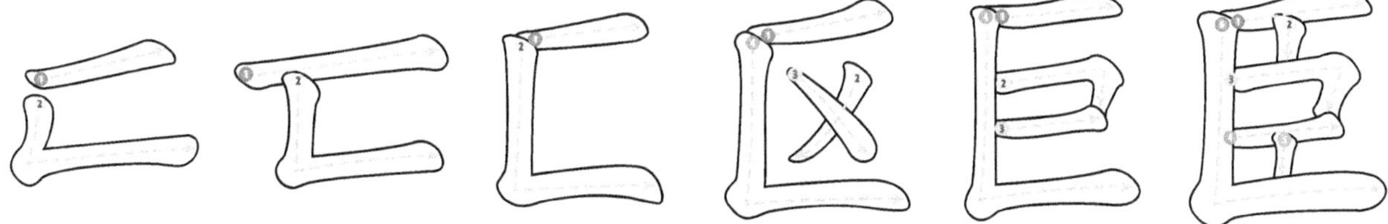

n-Frame

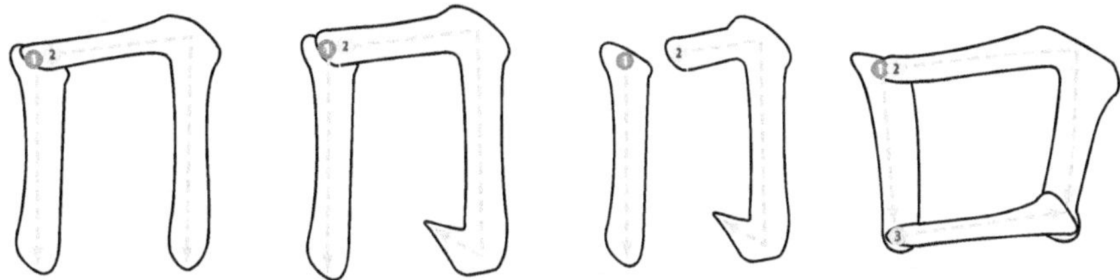

L7-Enclosure

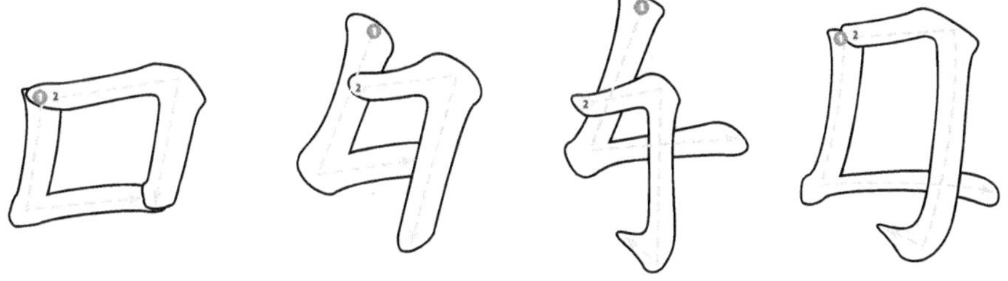

Single Leg

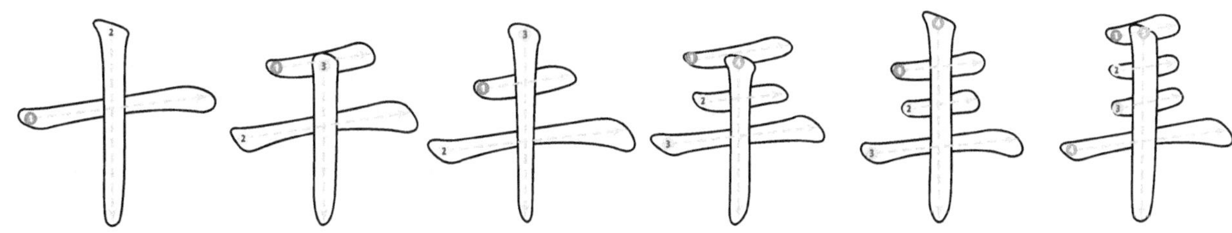

Multiple Legs

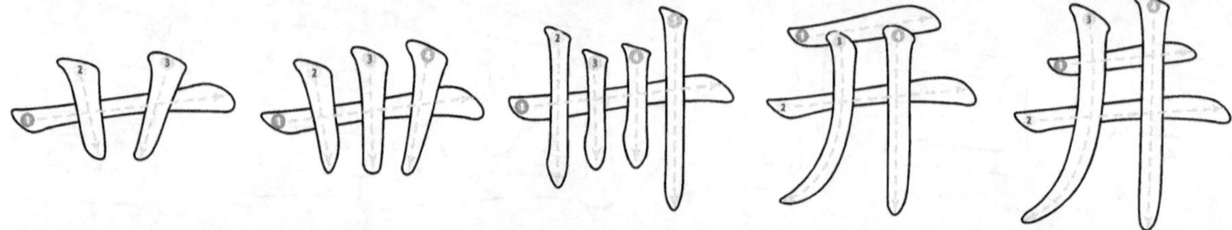

Split Intersections

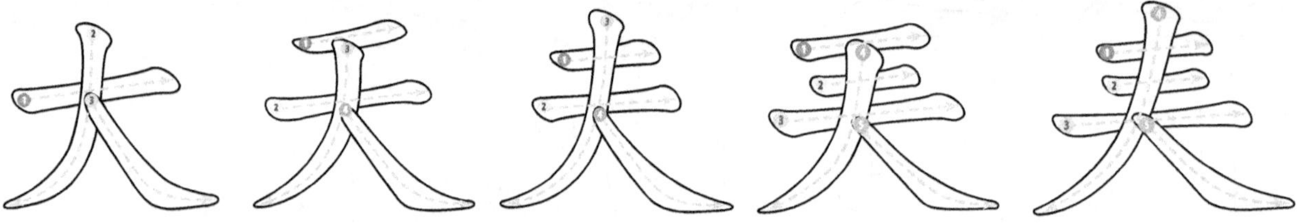

Tripod

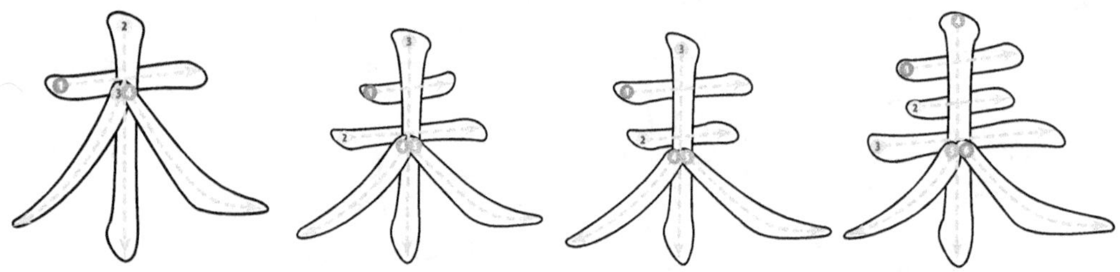

Flat Intersections

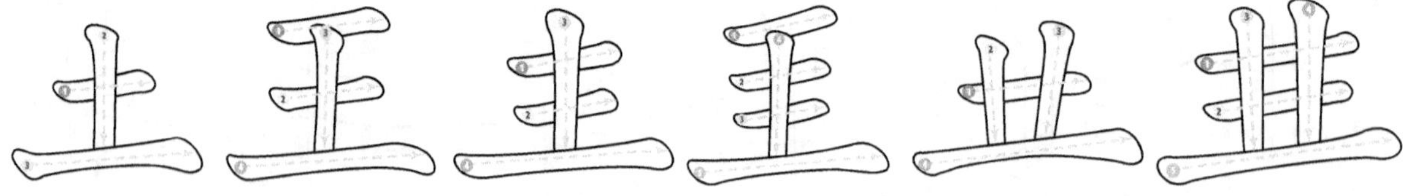

Skewer

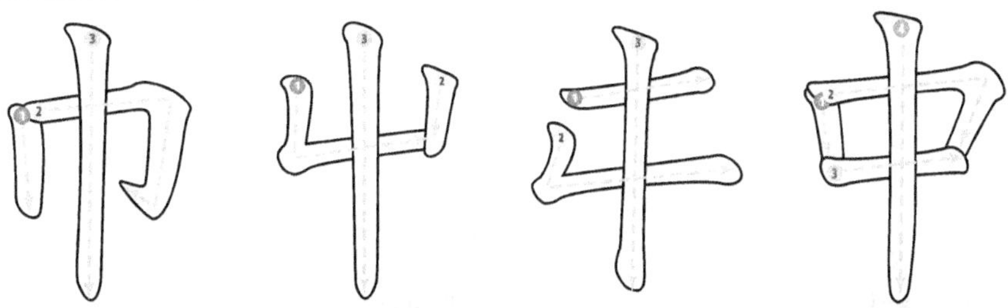

Horizontals Enclosure

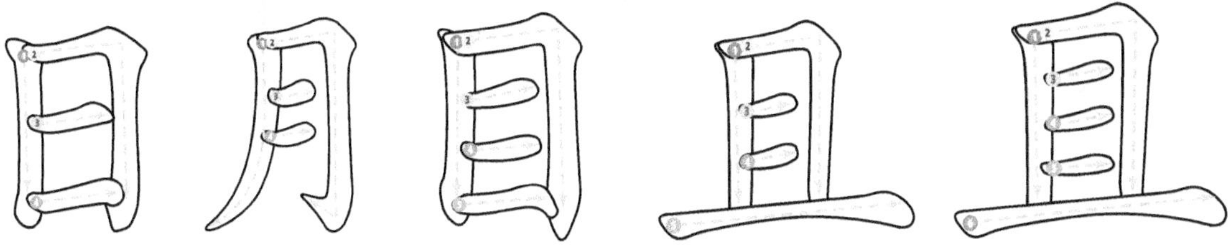

Verticals Enclosure

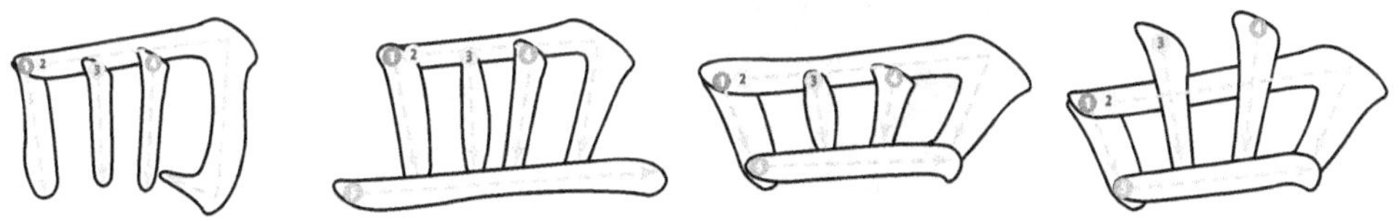

Intersections Enclosure

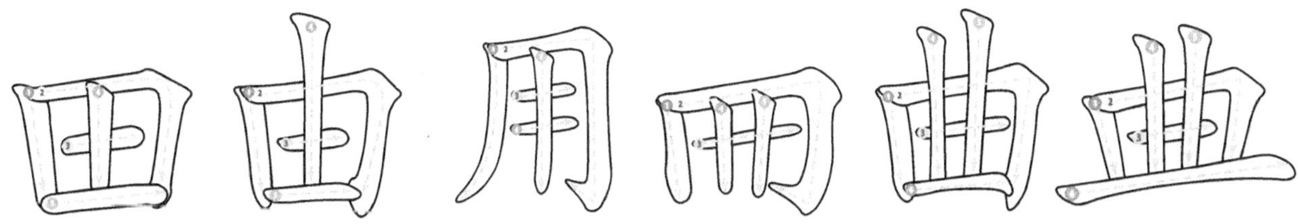

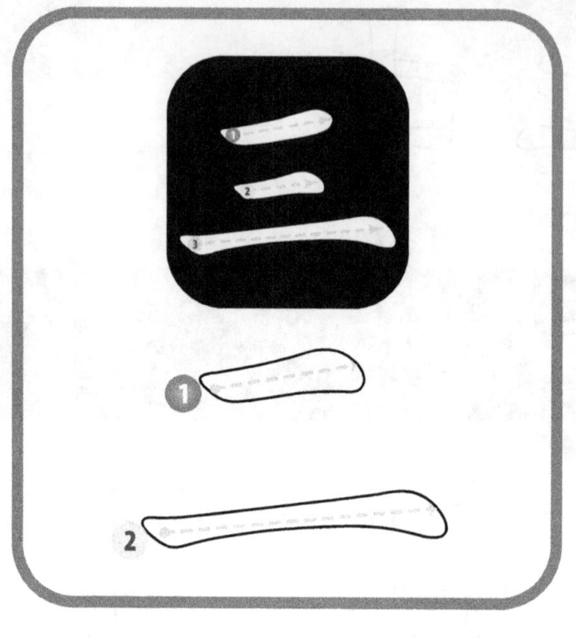

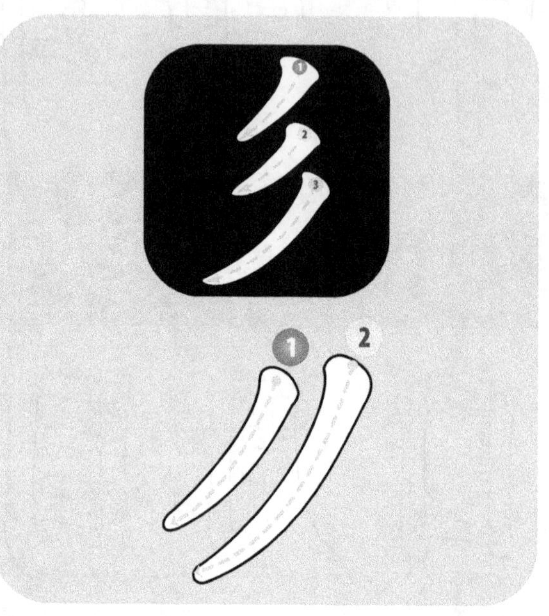

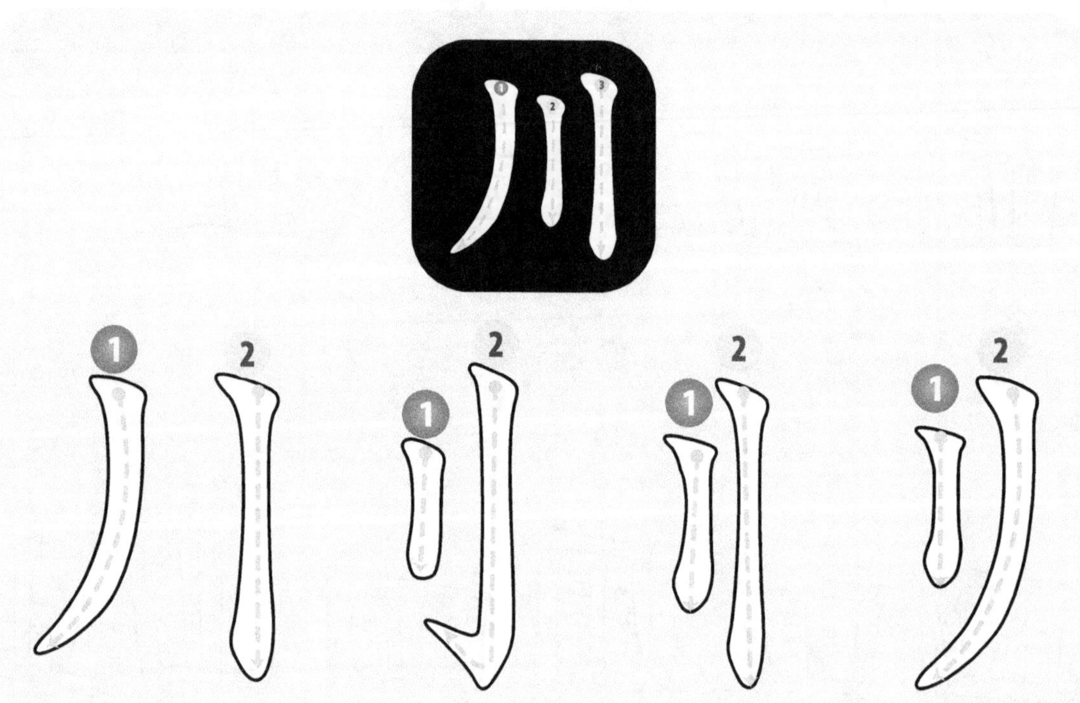

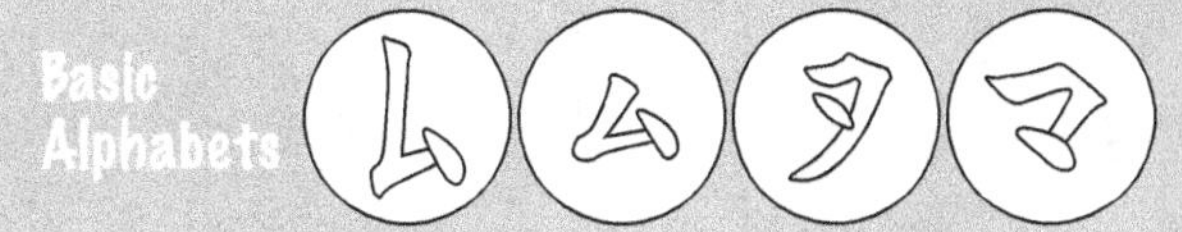
ム ム タ マ

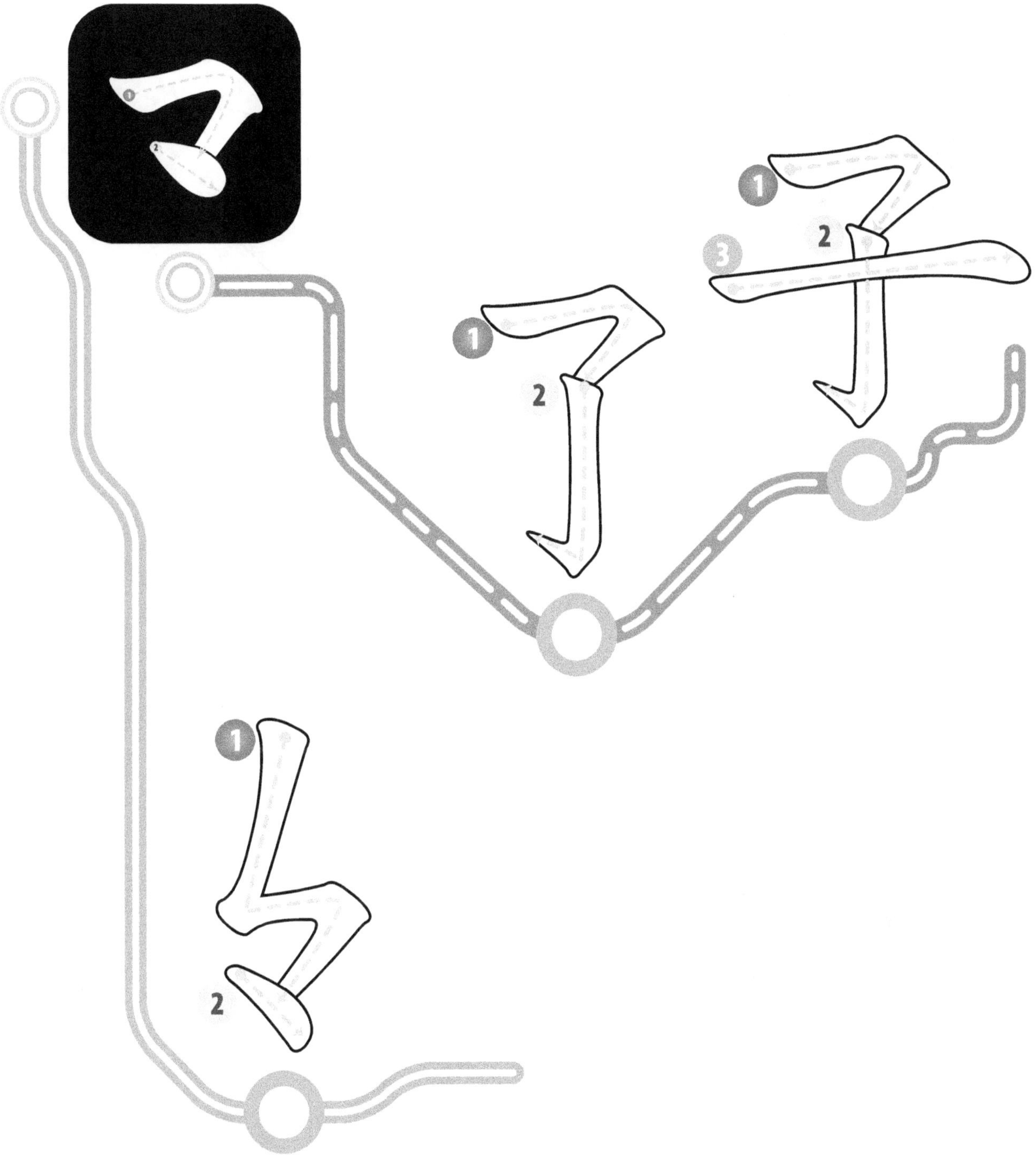

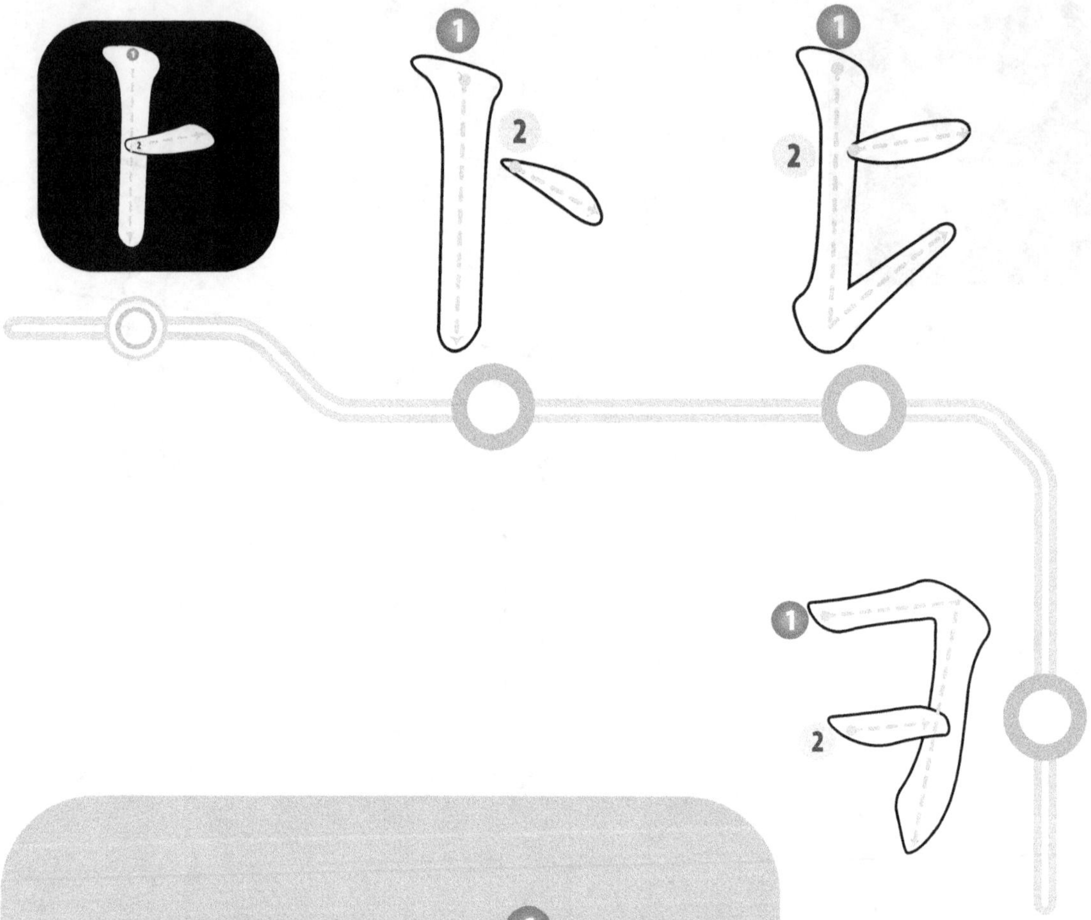

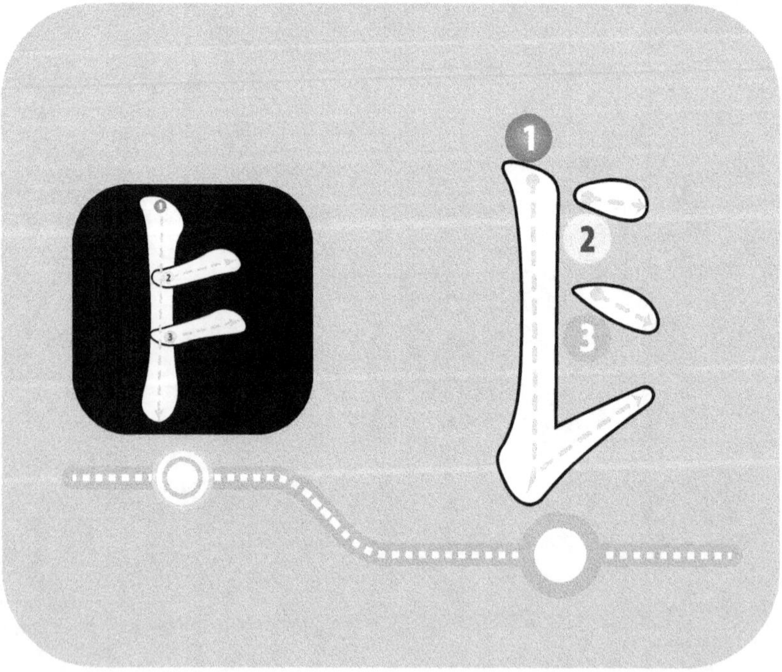

Half Ladder
Variations

Basic Alphabets

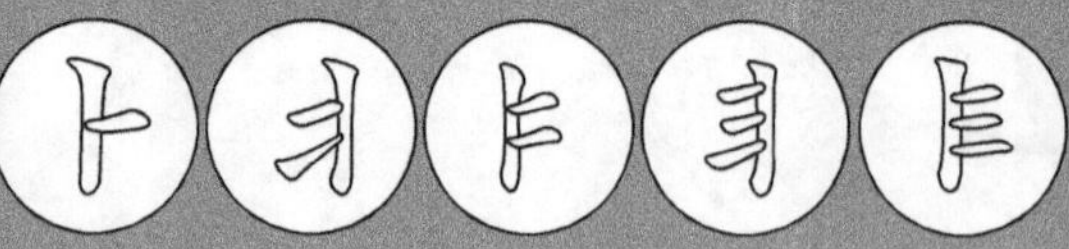

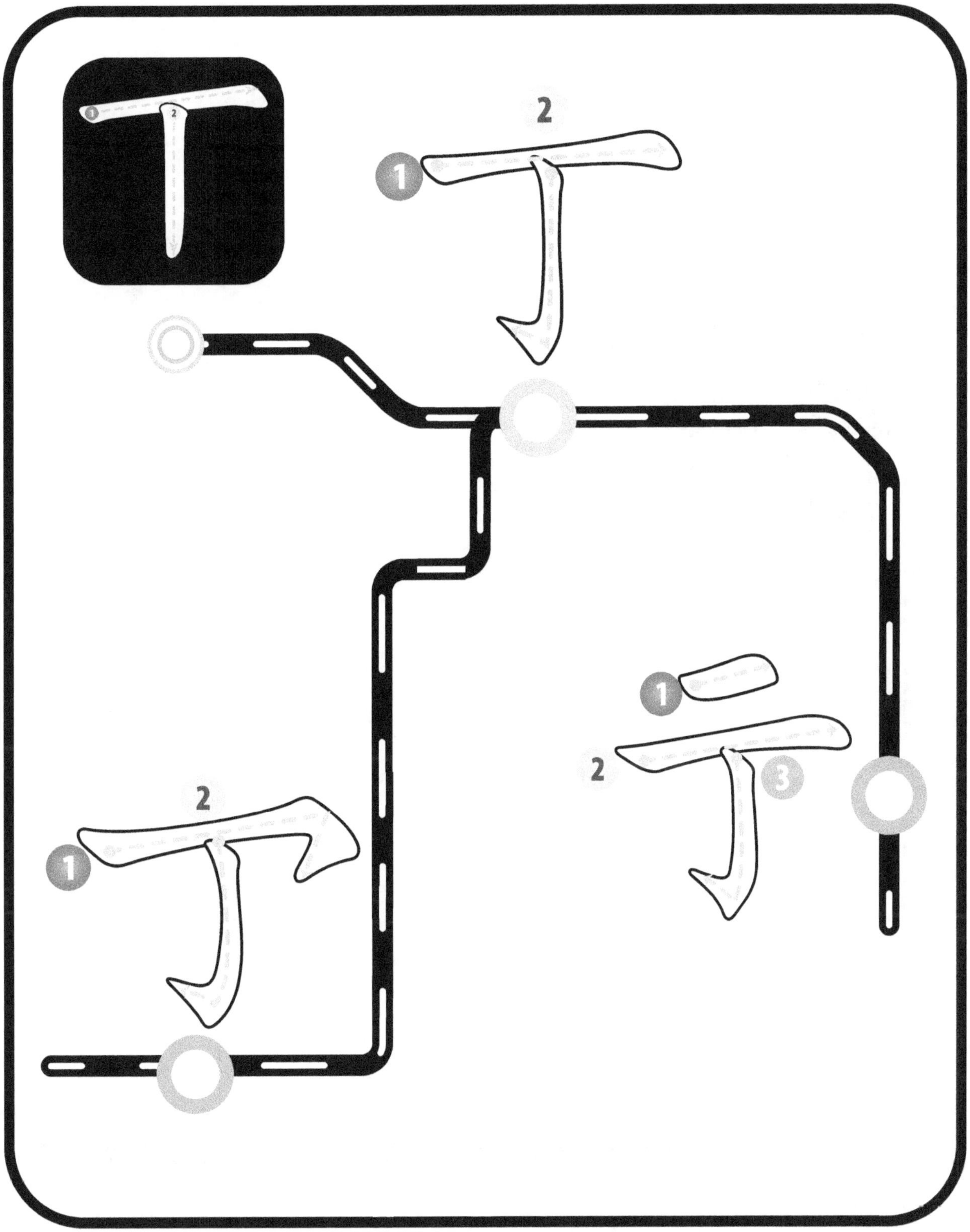

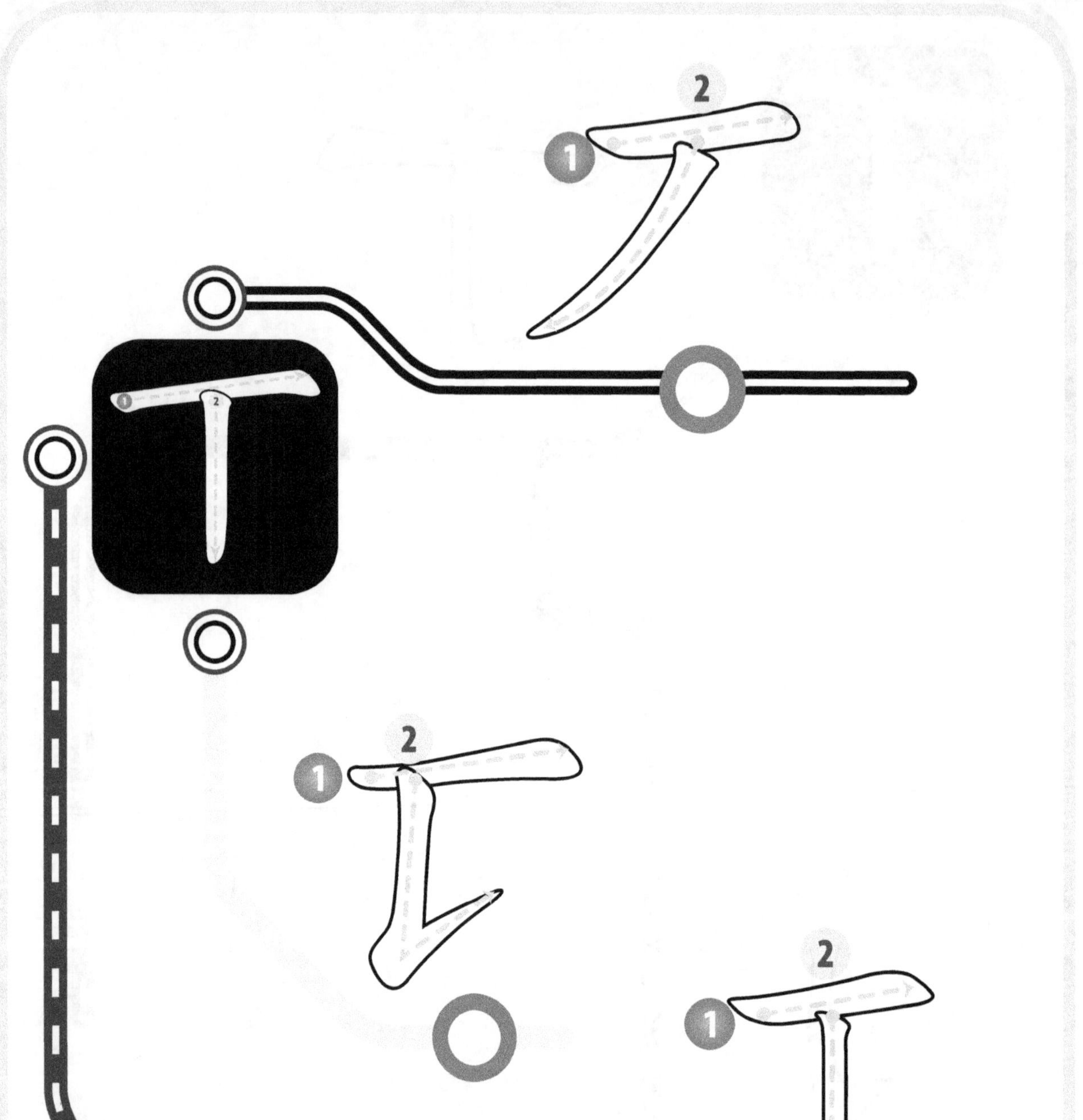

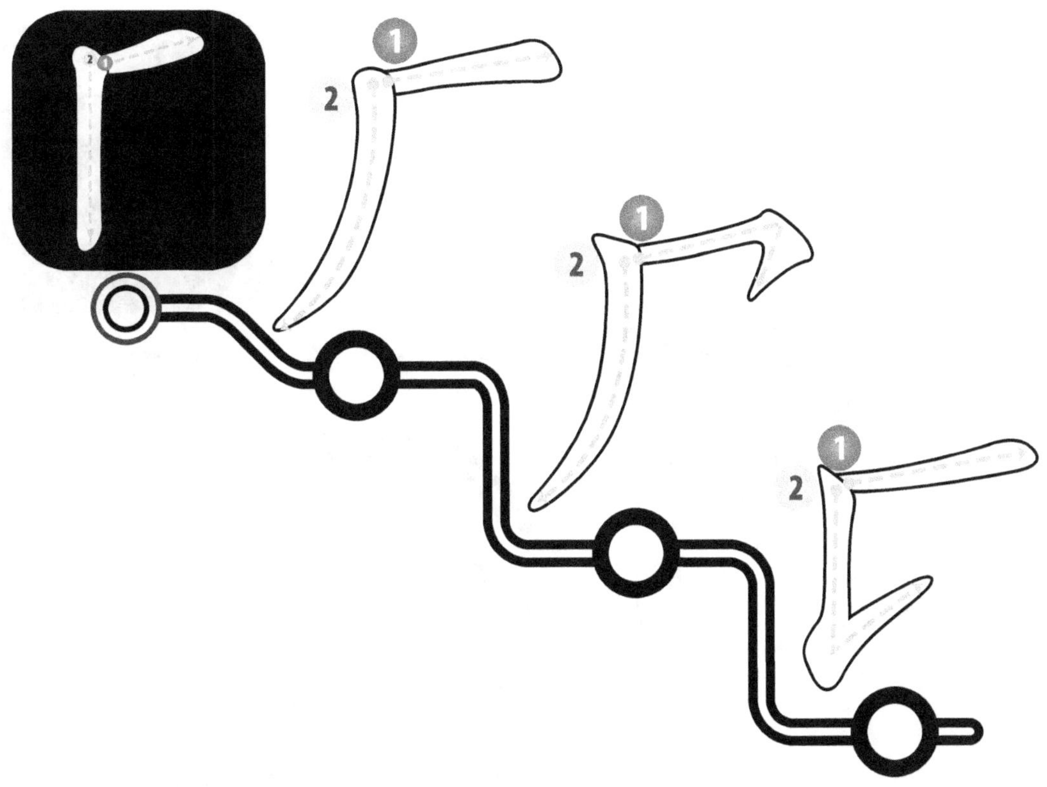

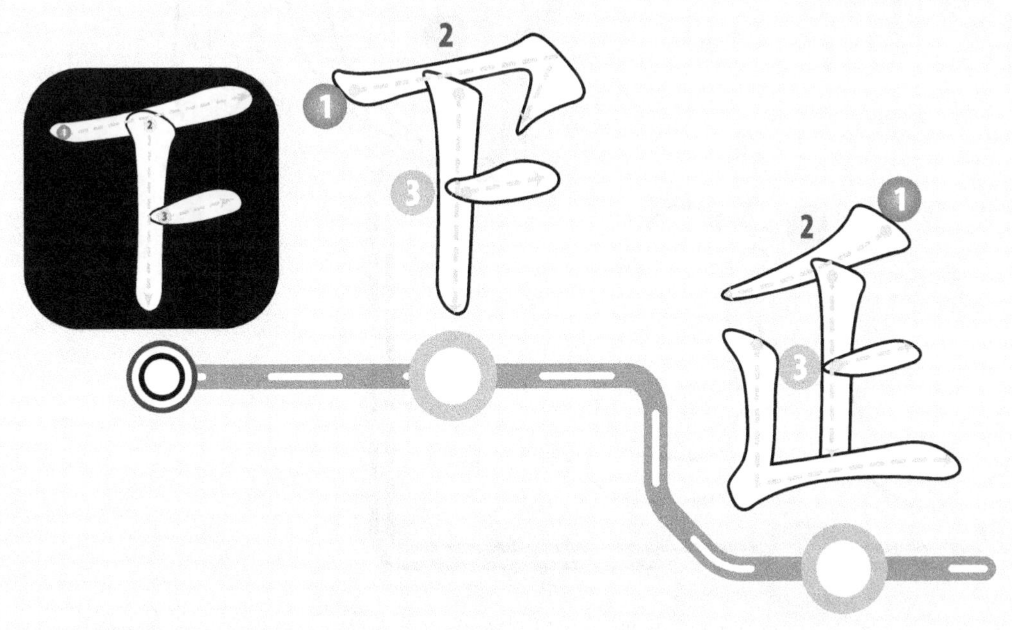

4C T-Shape Variations

Basic Alphabets

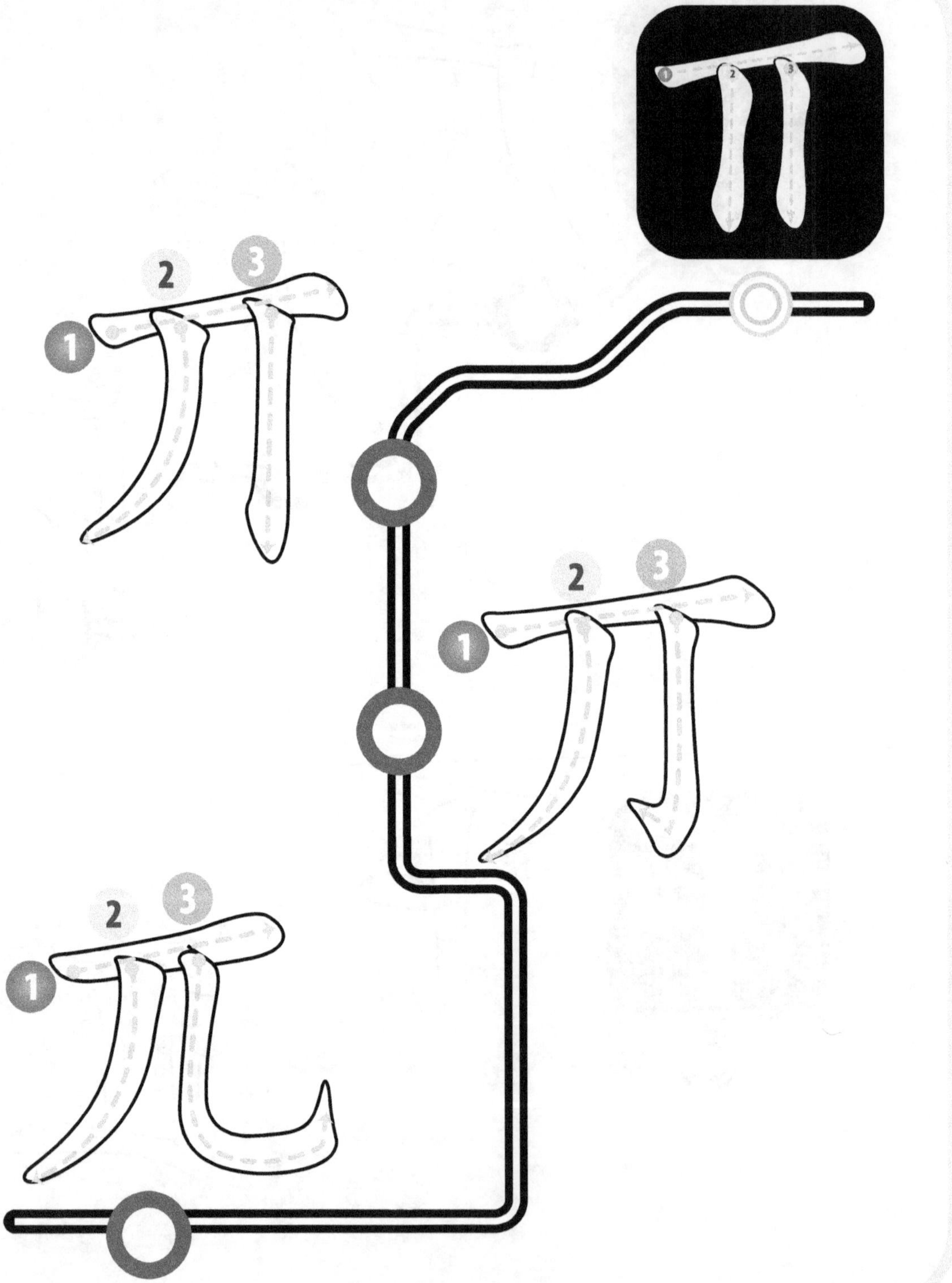

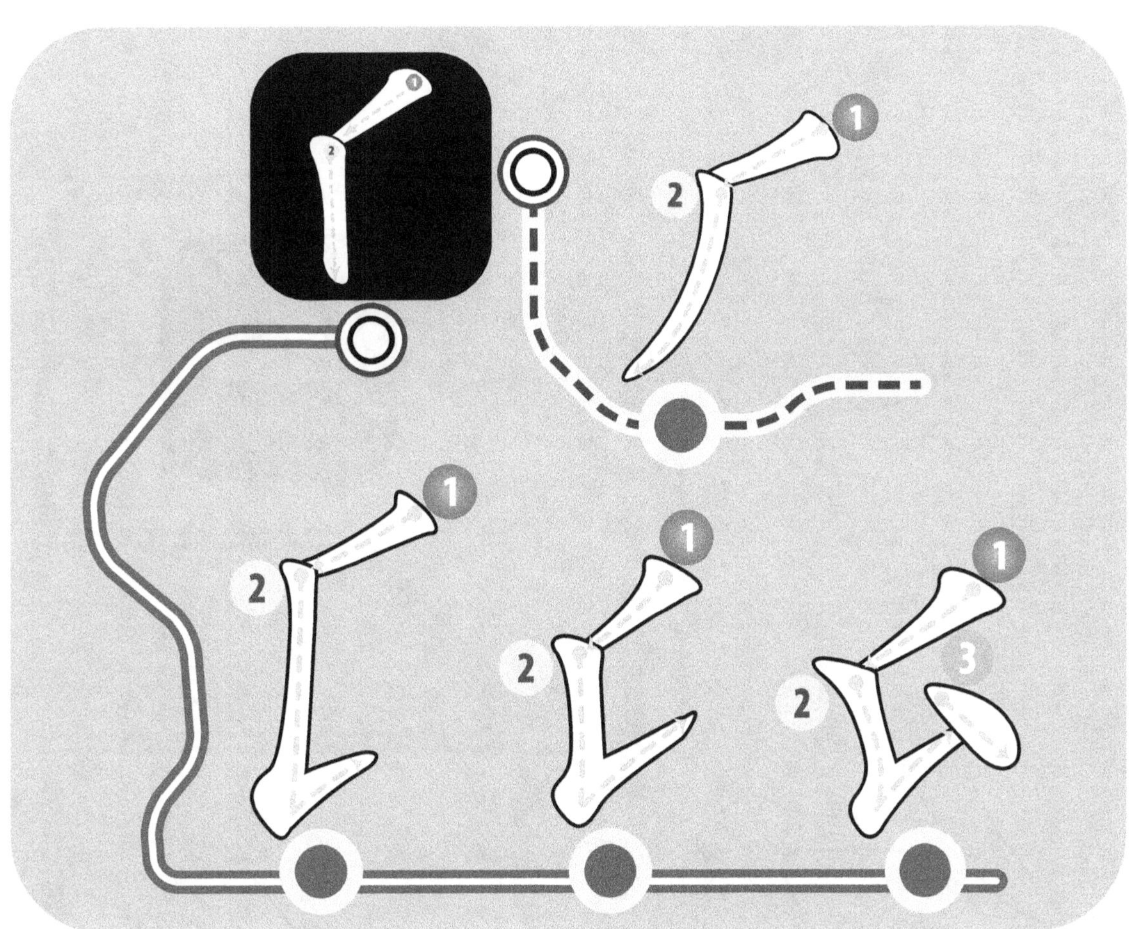

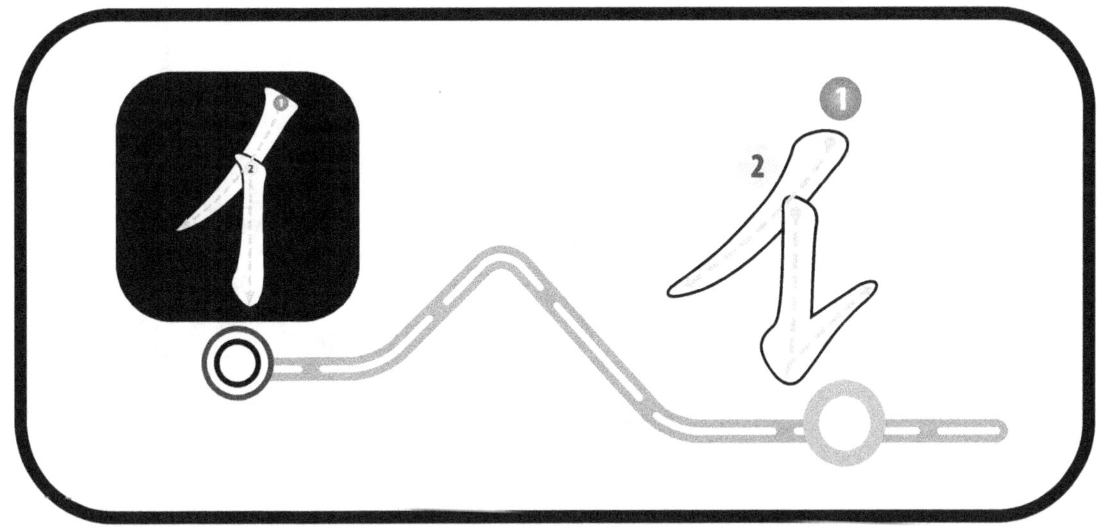

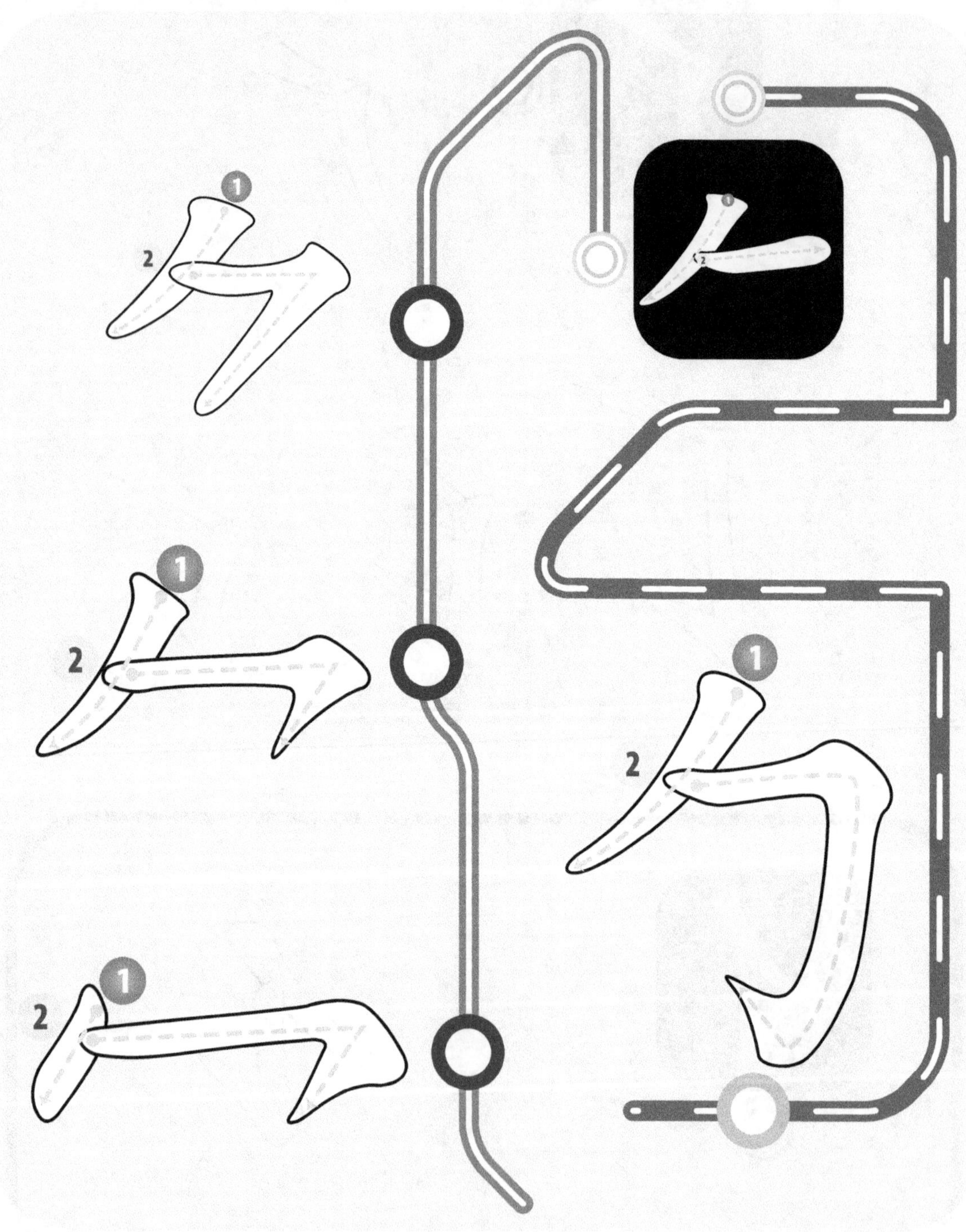

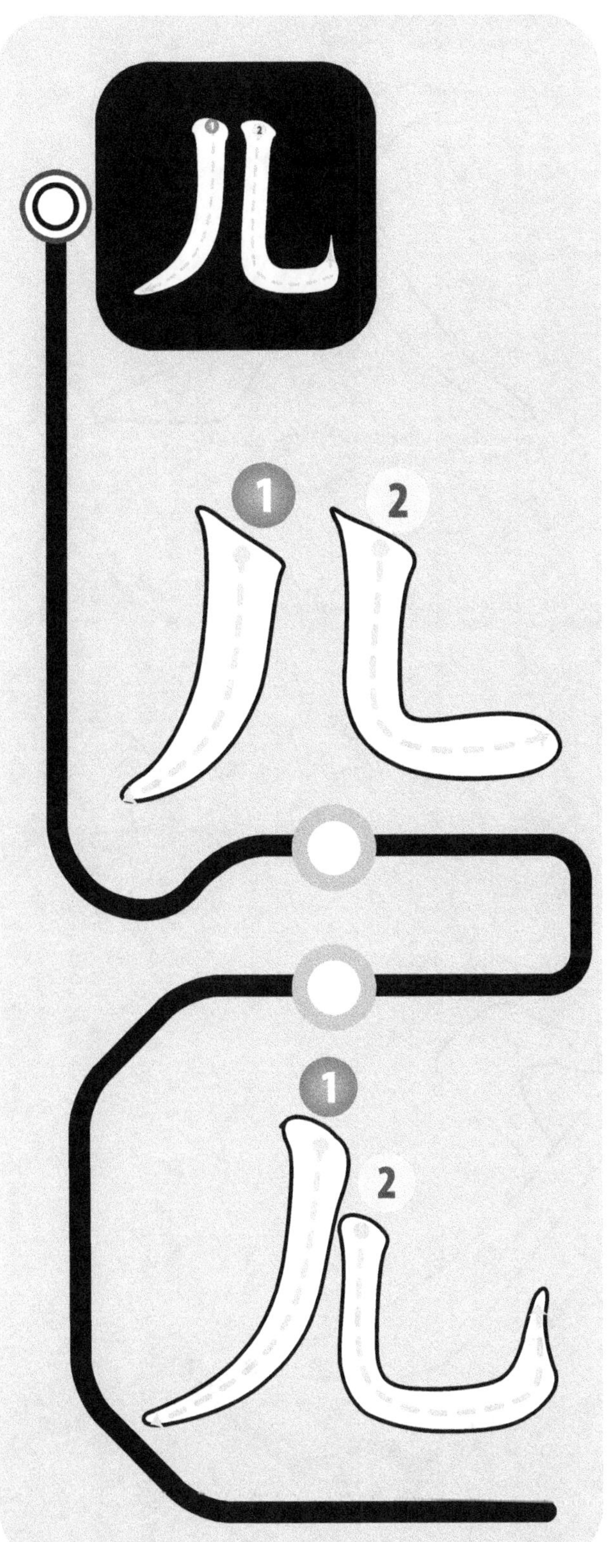

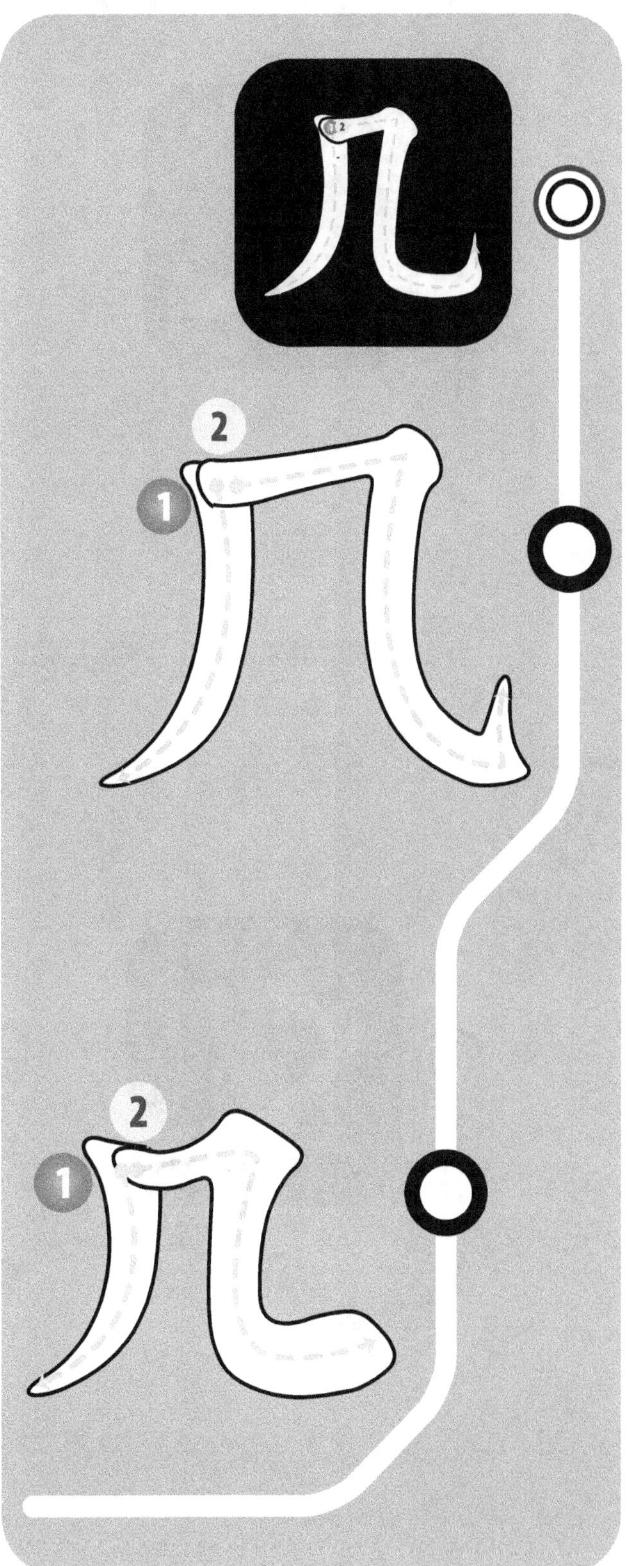

7
Split
Variation

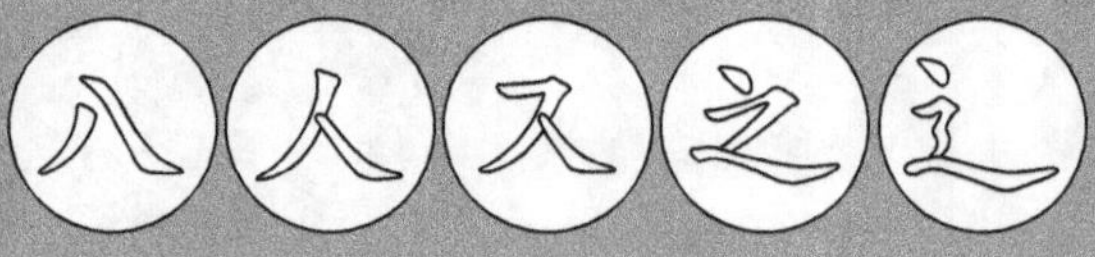

Basic
Alphabets

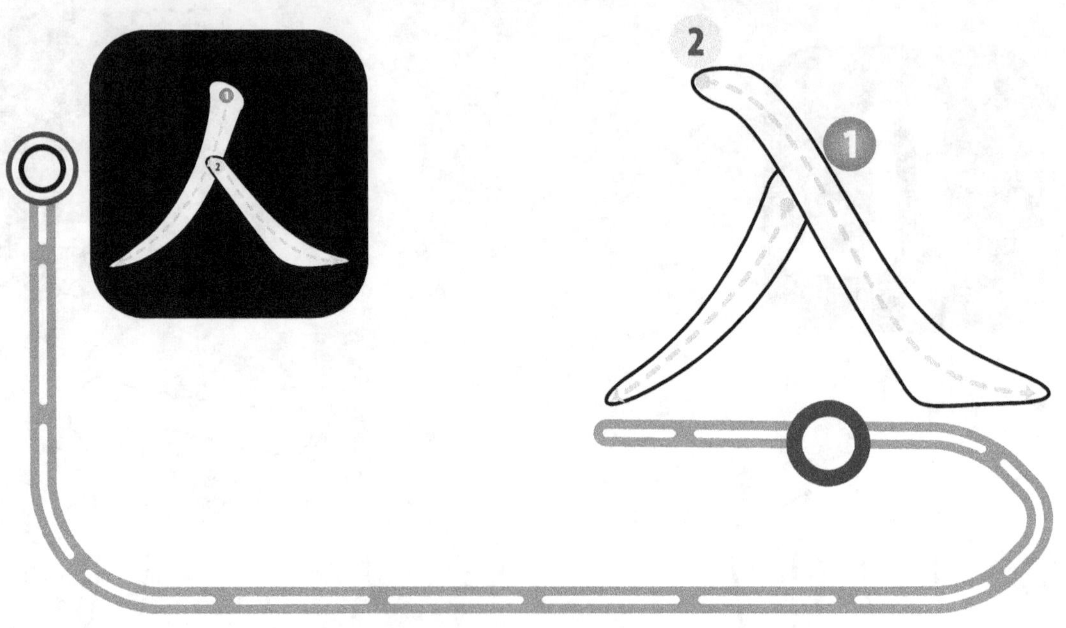

2
1

8
Slide
Variation

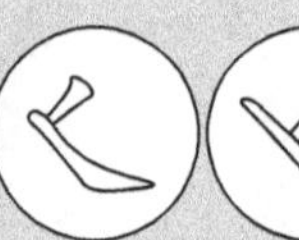

Basic
Alphabets

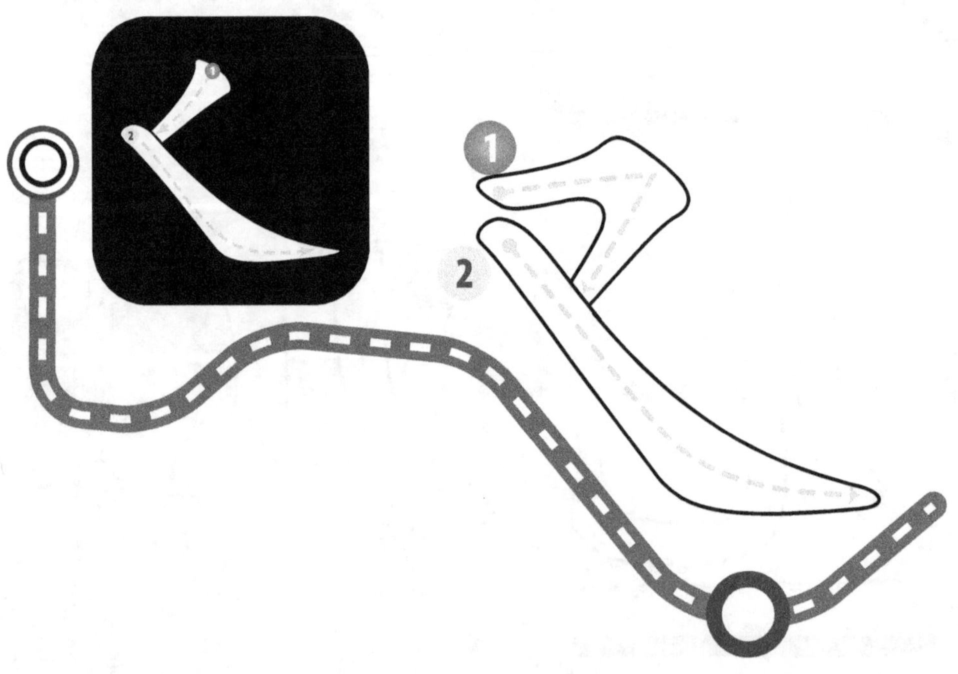

1
2

9
Basic Alphabets
ㄗ ㄗ ㄗ
7-Hook Flag Variations

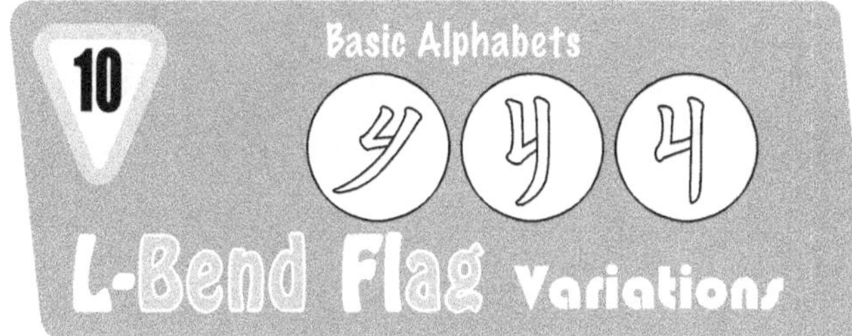

10
Basic Alphabets
ㄙ ㄙ ㄙ
L-Bend Flag Variations

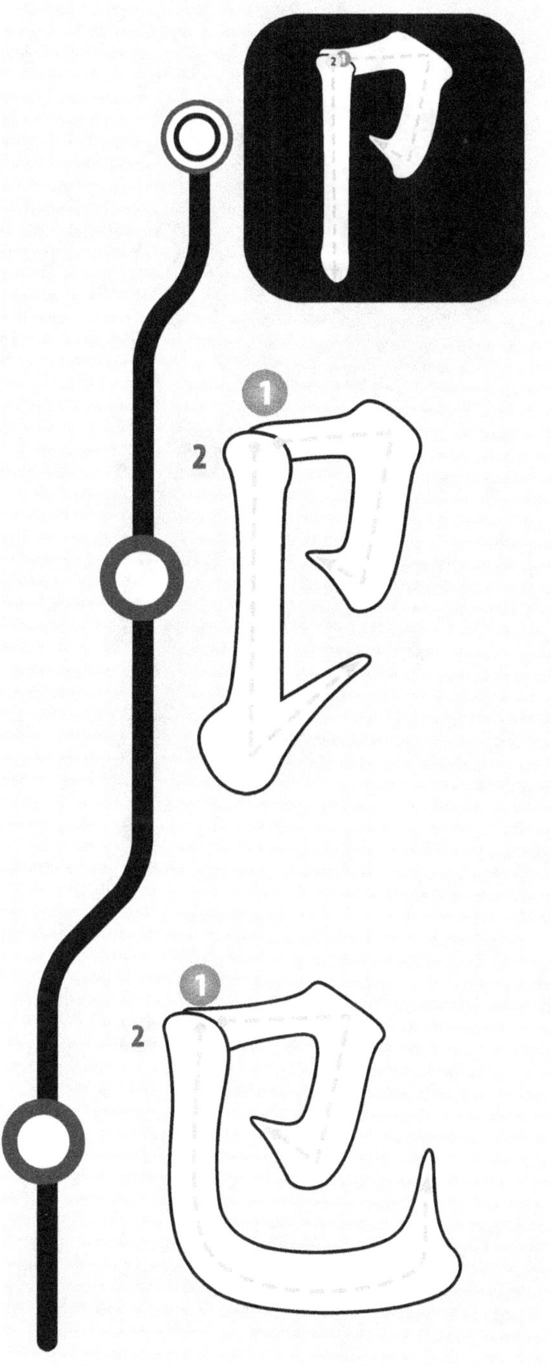

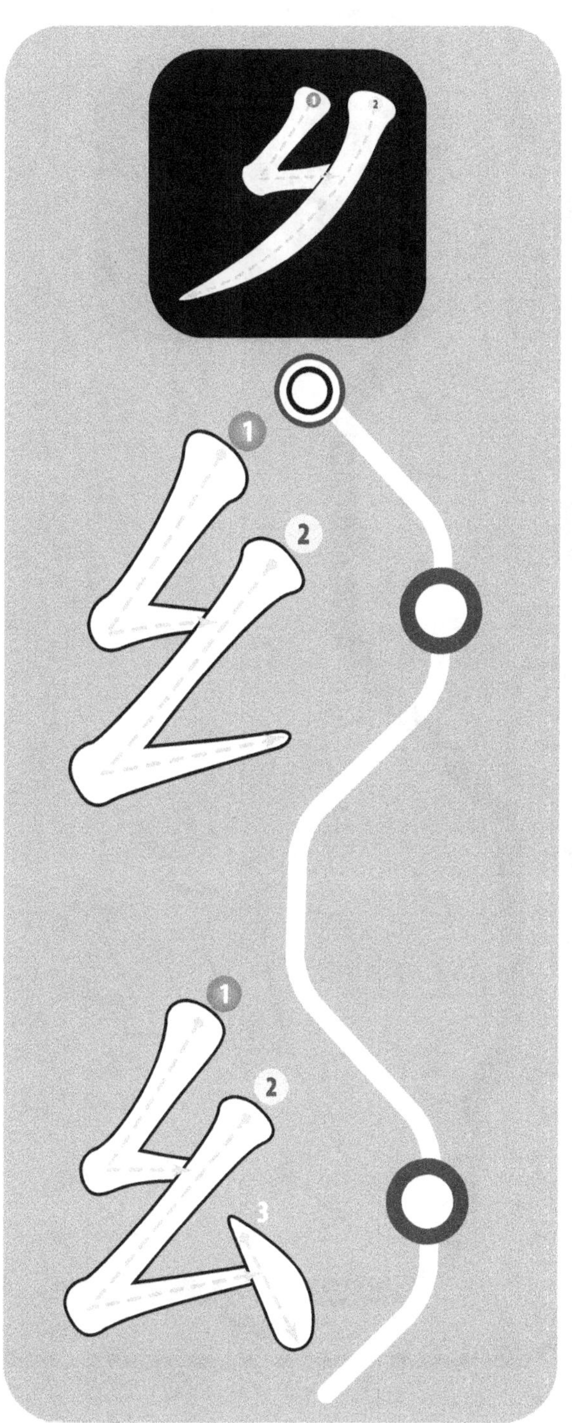

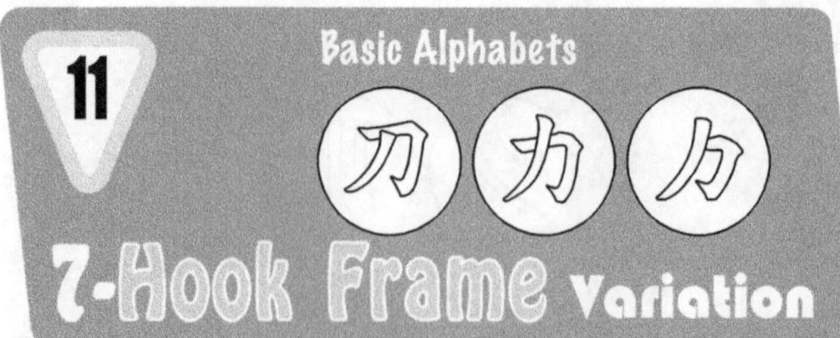

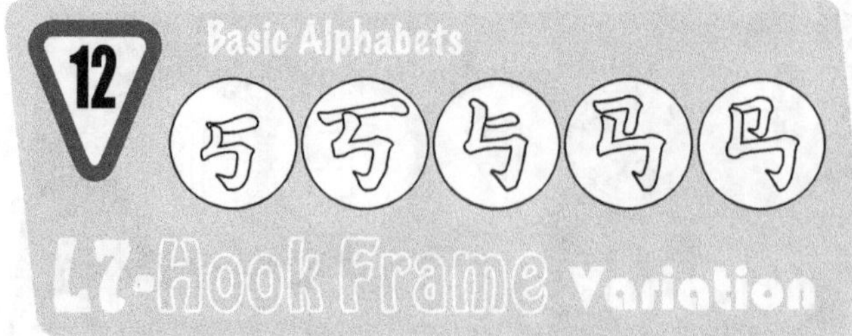

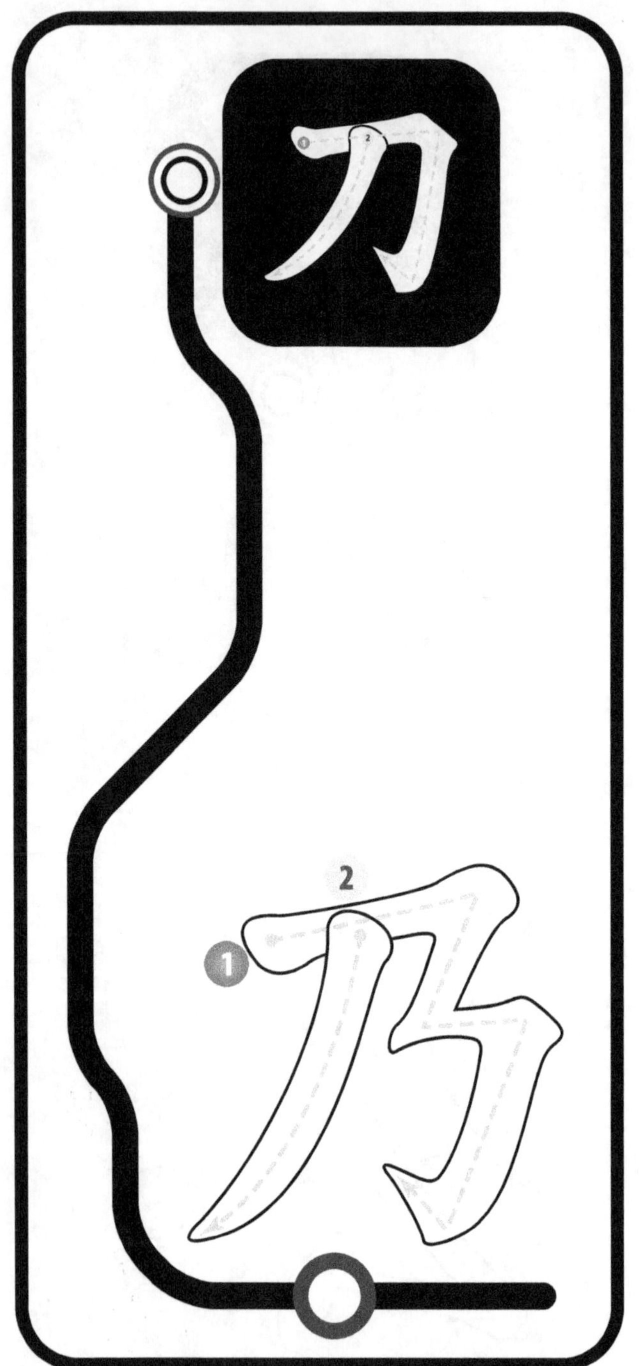

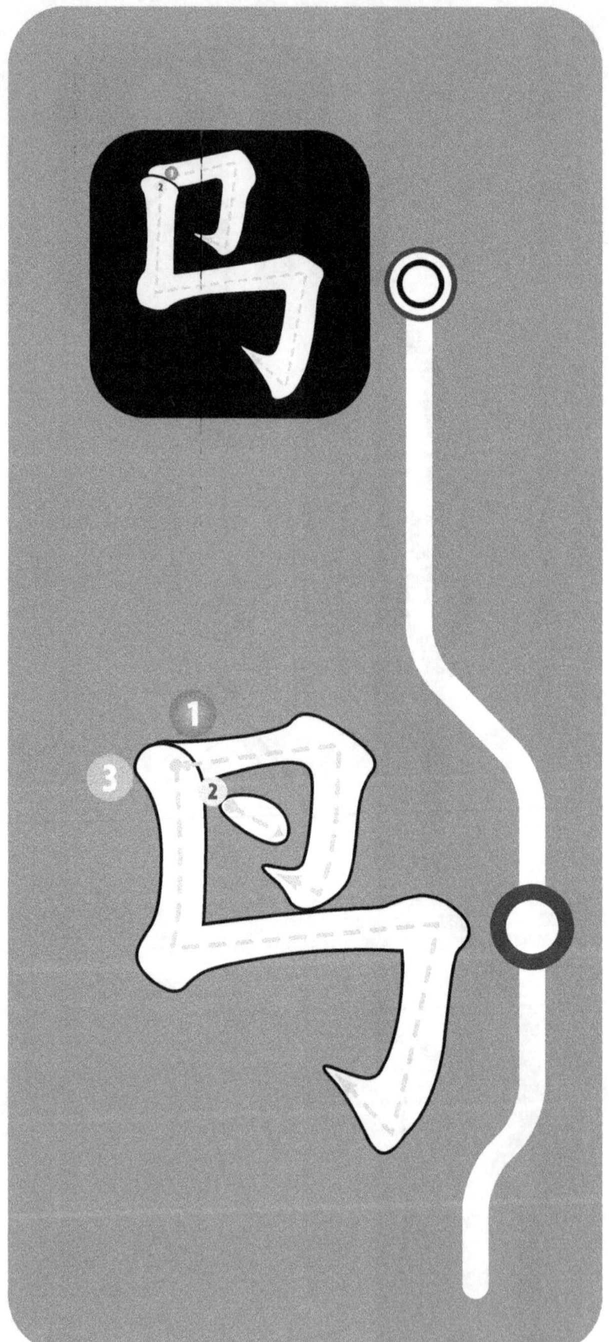

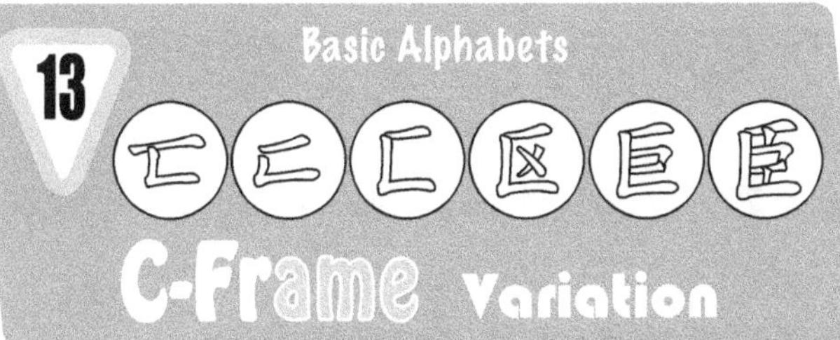
C-Frame Variation

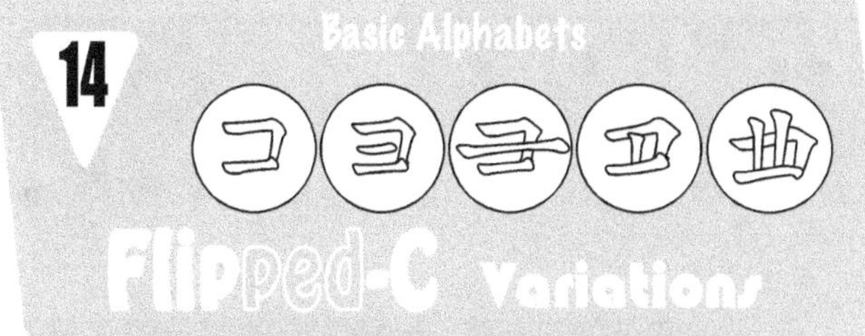
Flipped-C Variations

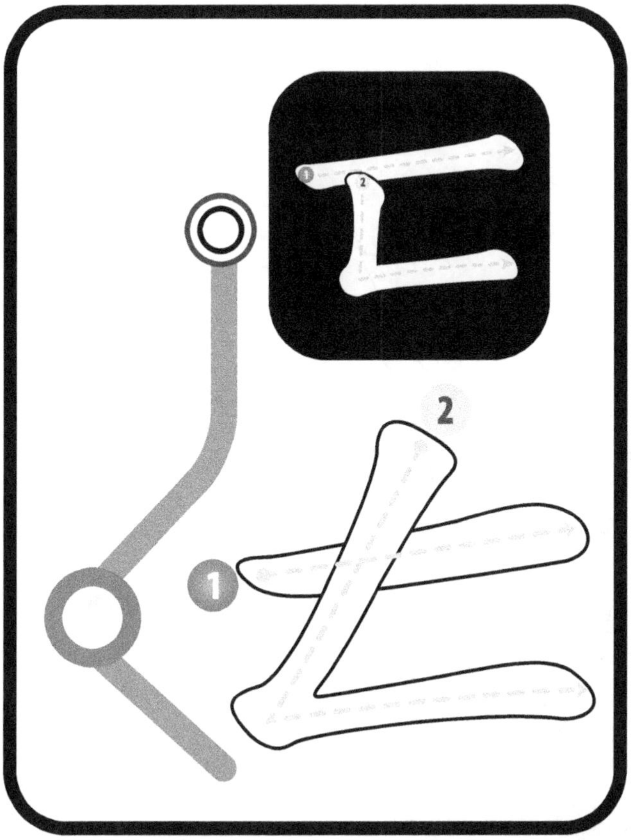

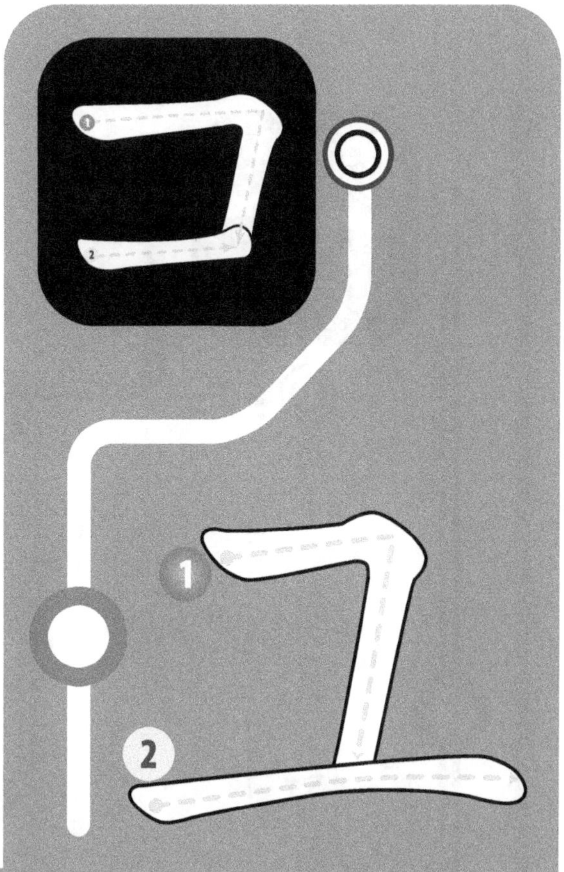

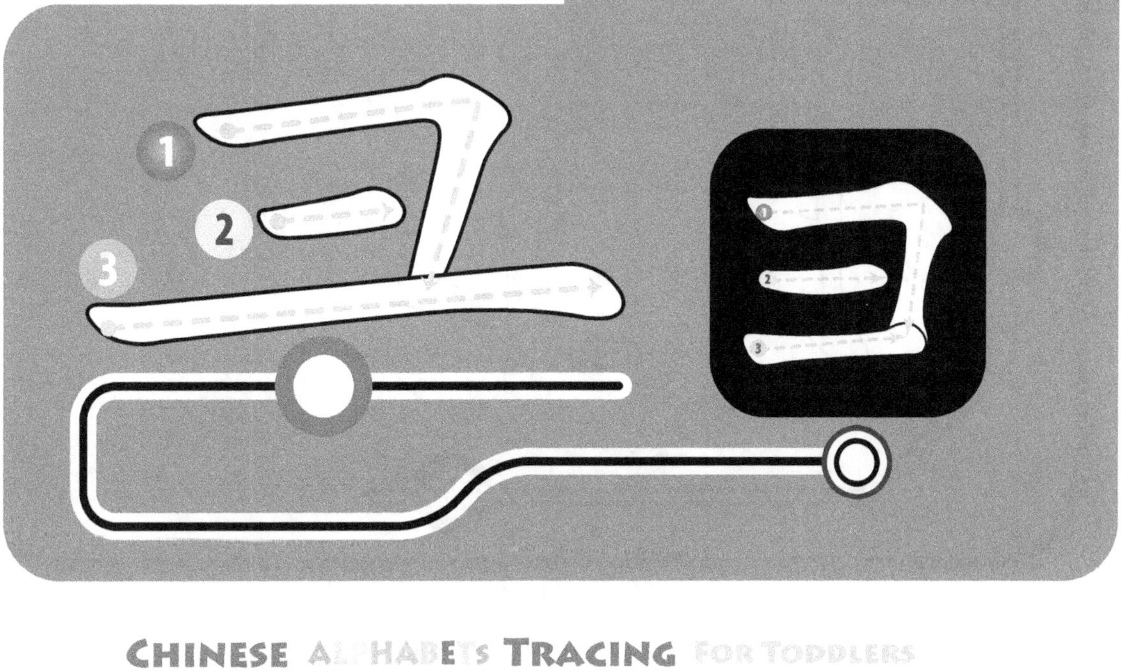

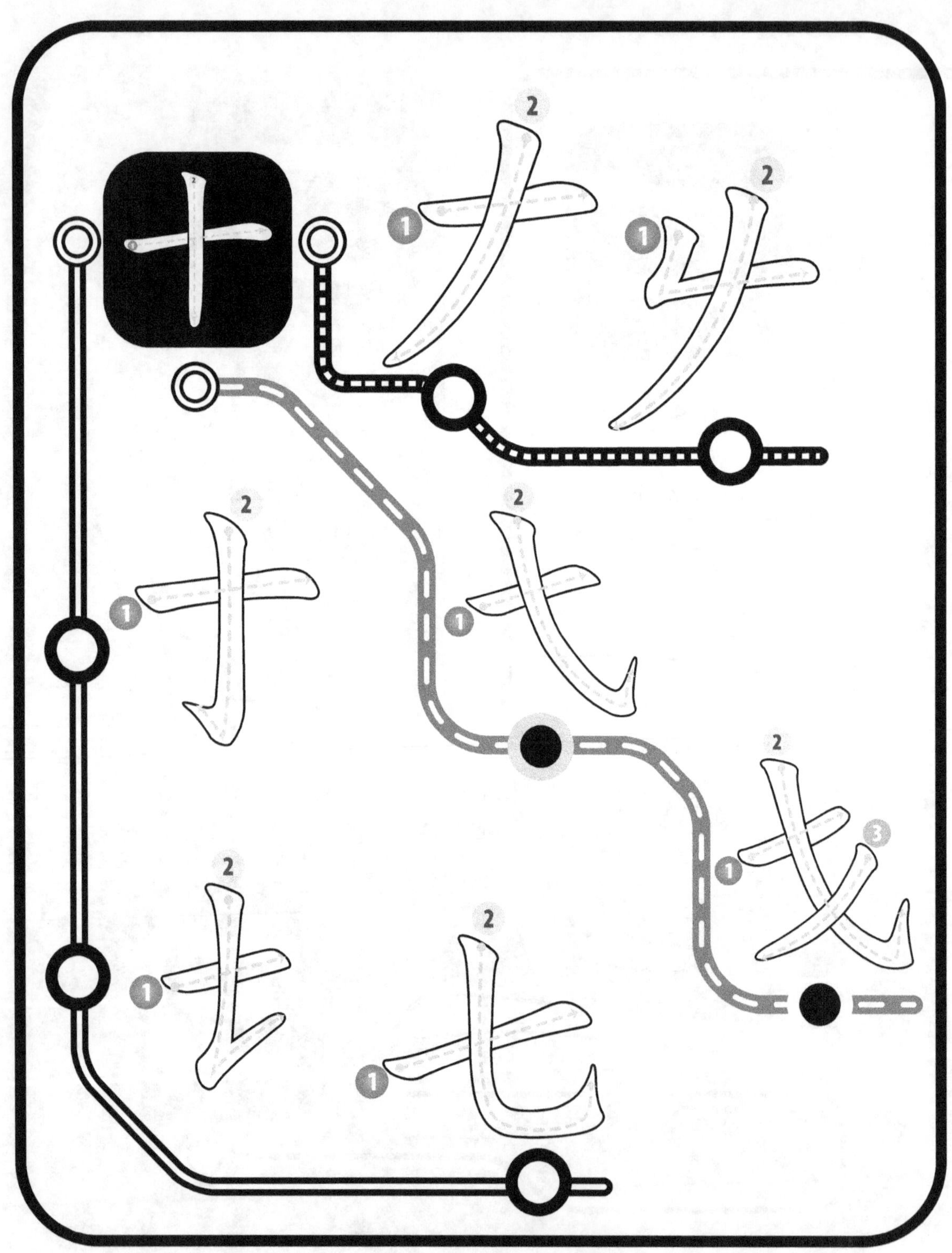

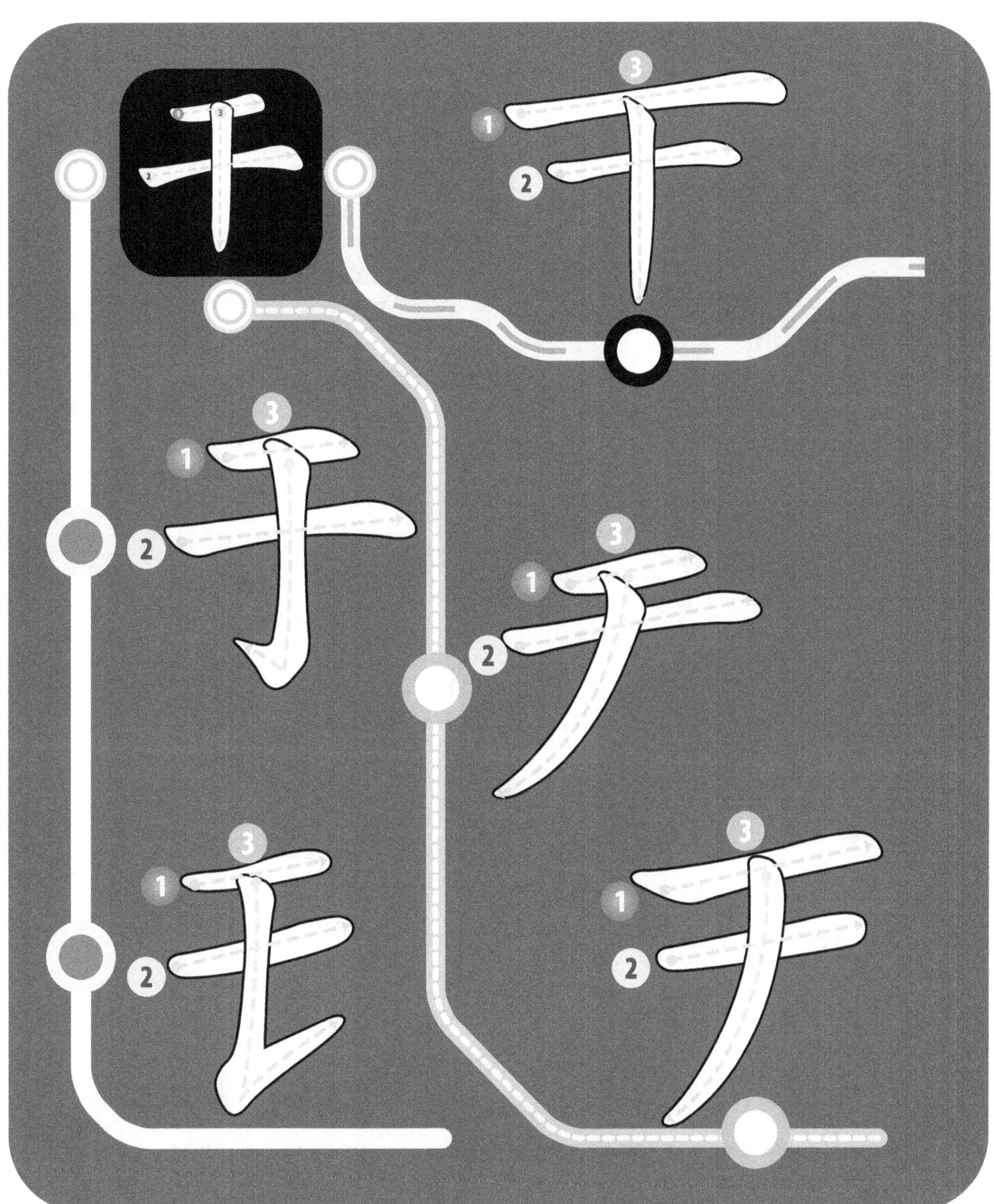

Single Leg Variations

Basic Alphabets

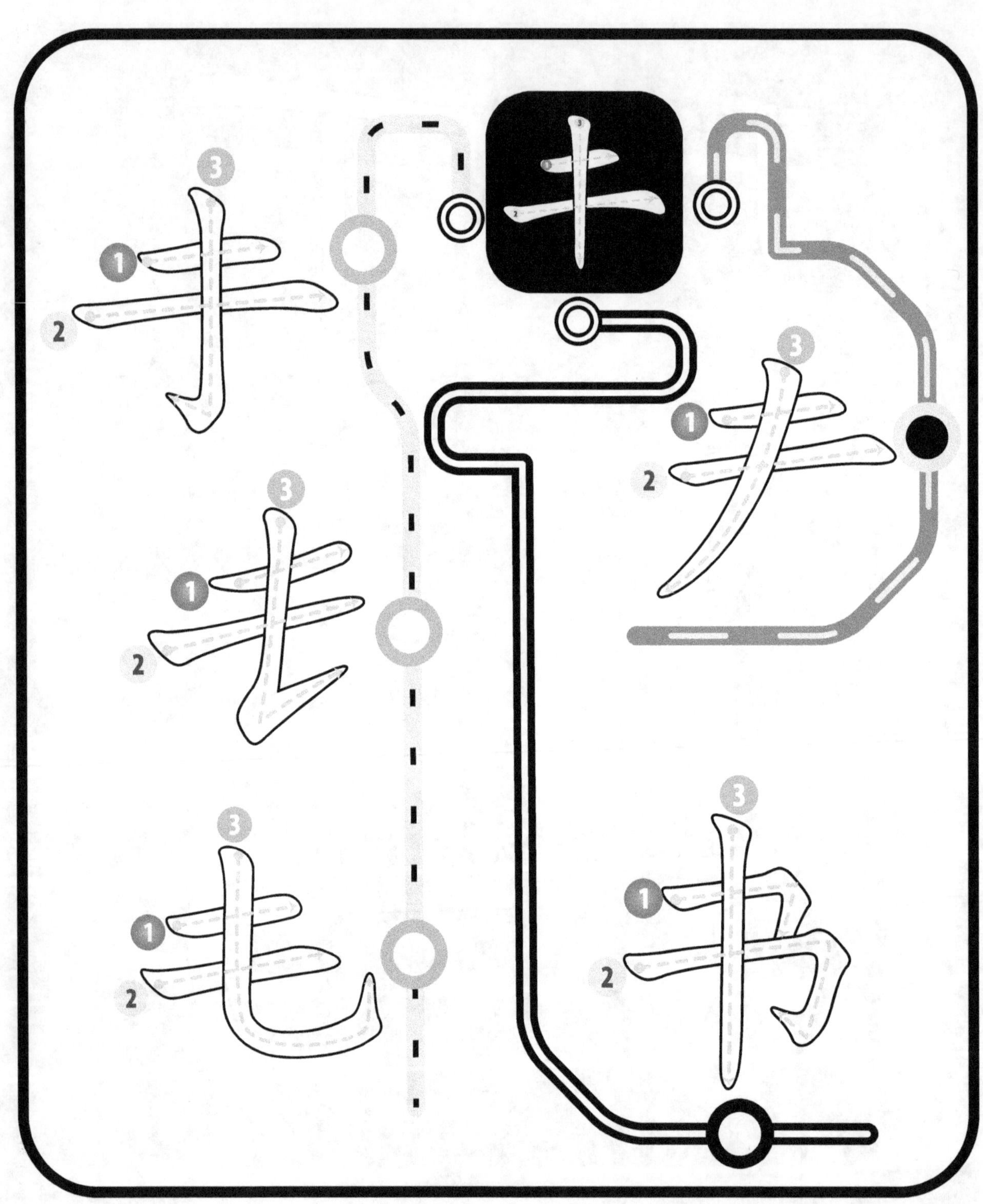

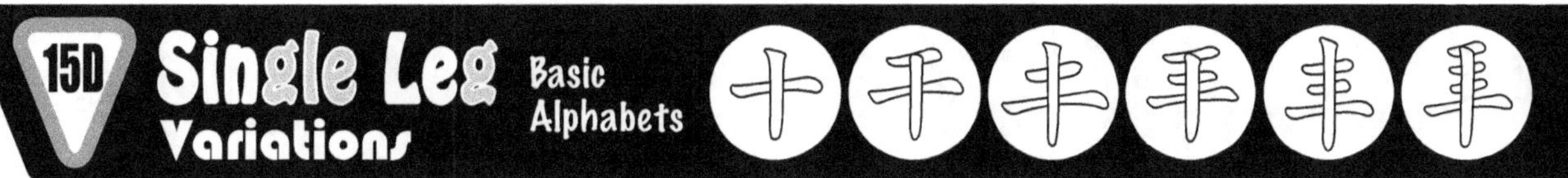

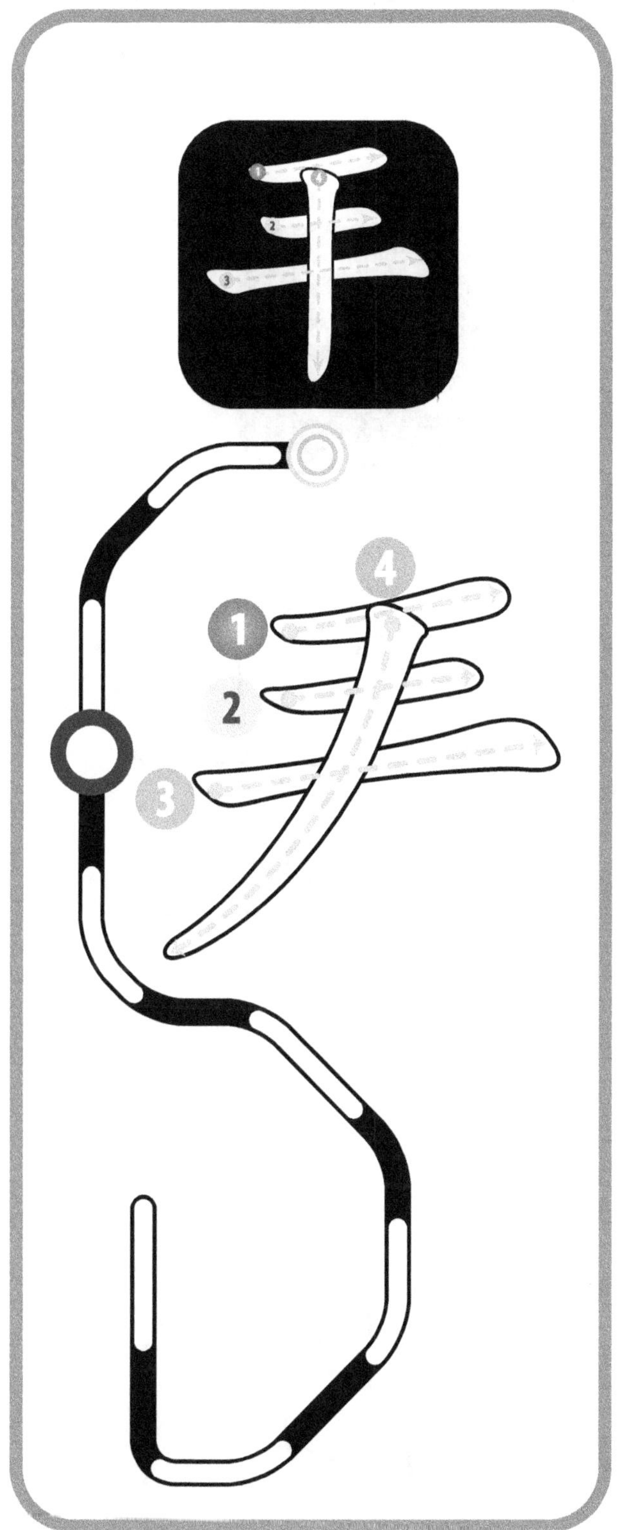

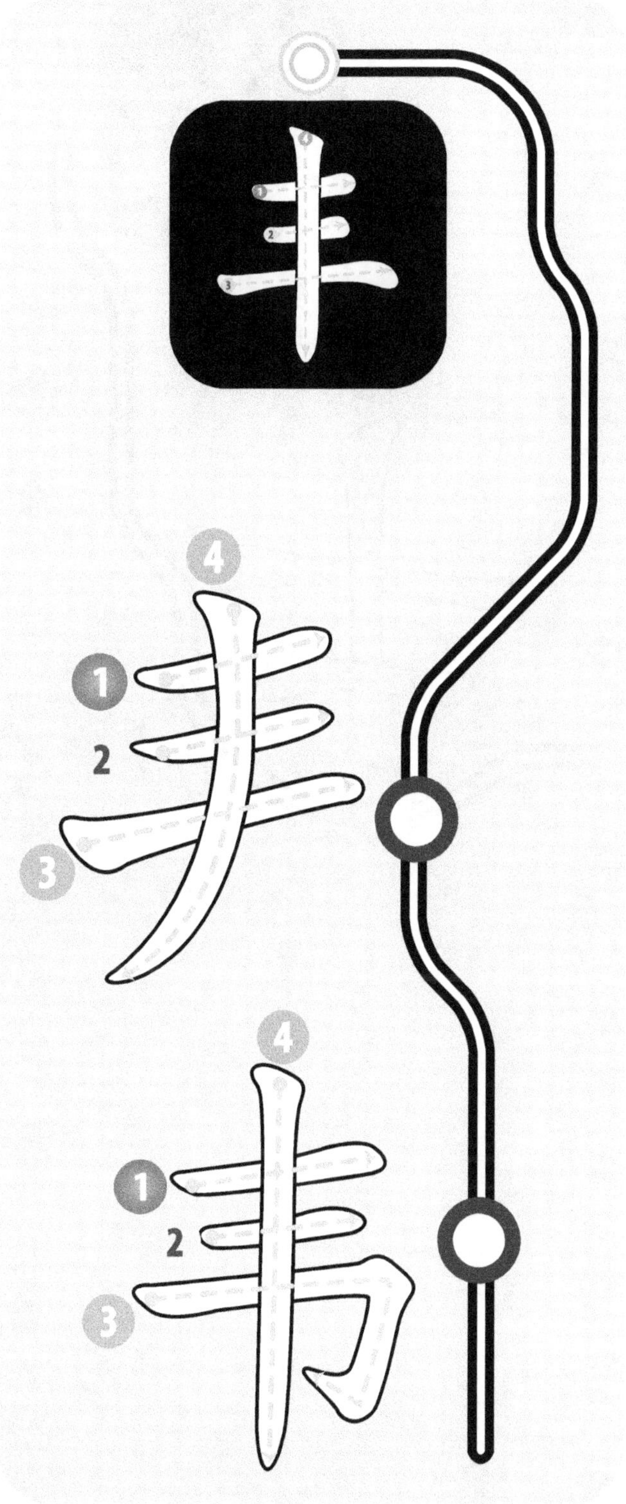

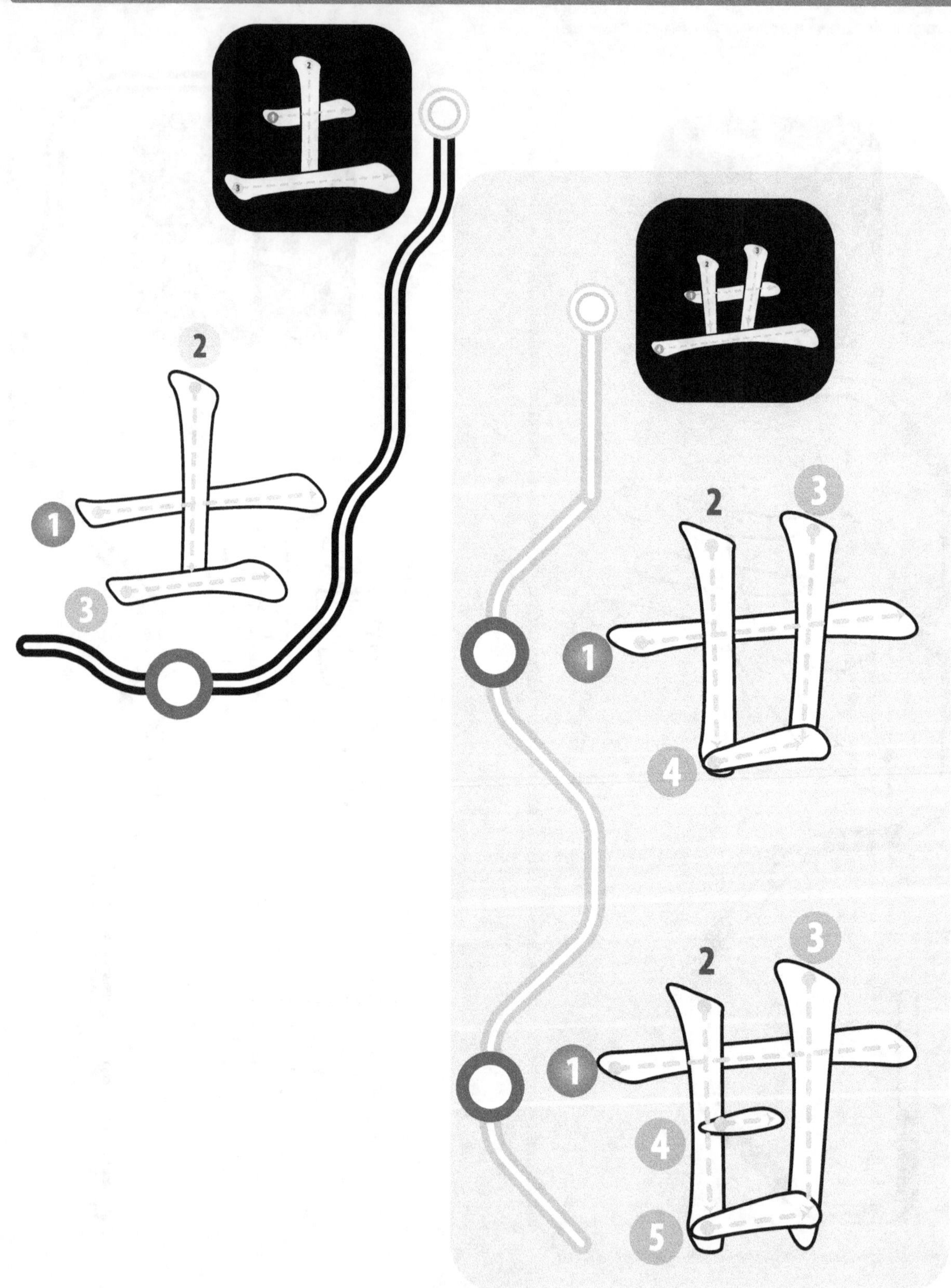

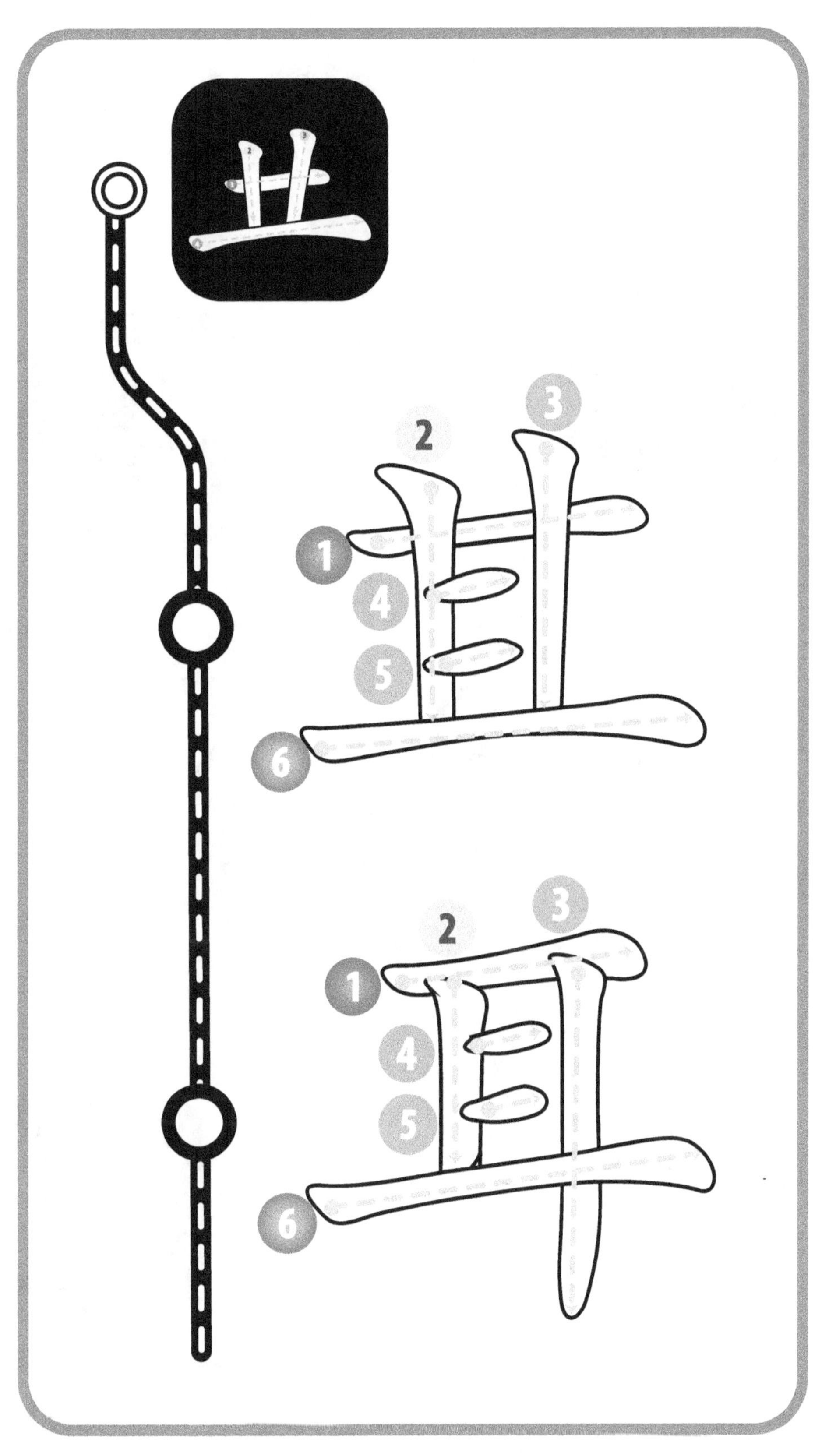

17
Basic Alphabets
Multiple Legs Variation

18
Basic Alphabets
n-Frame Variations

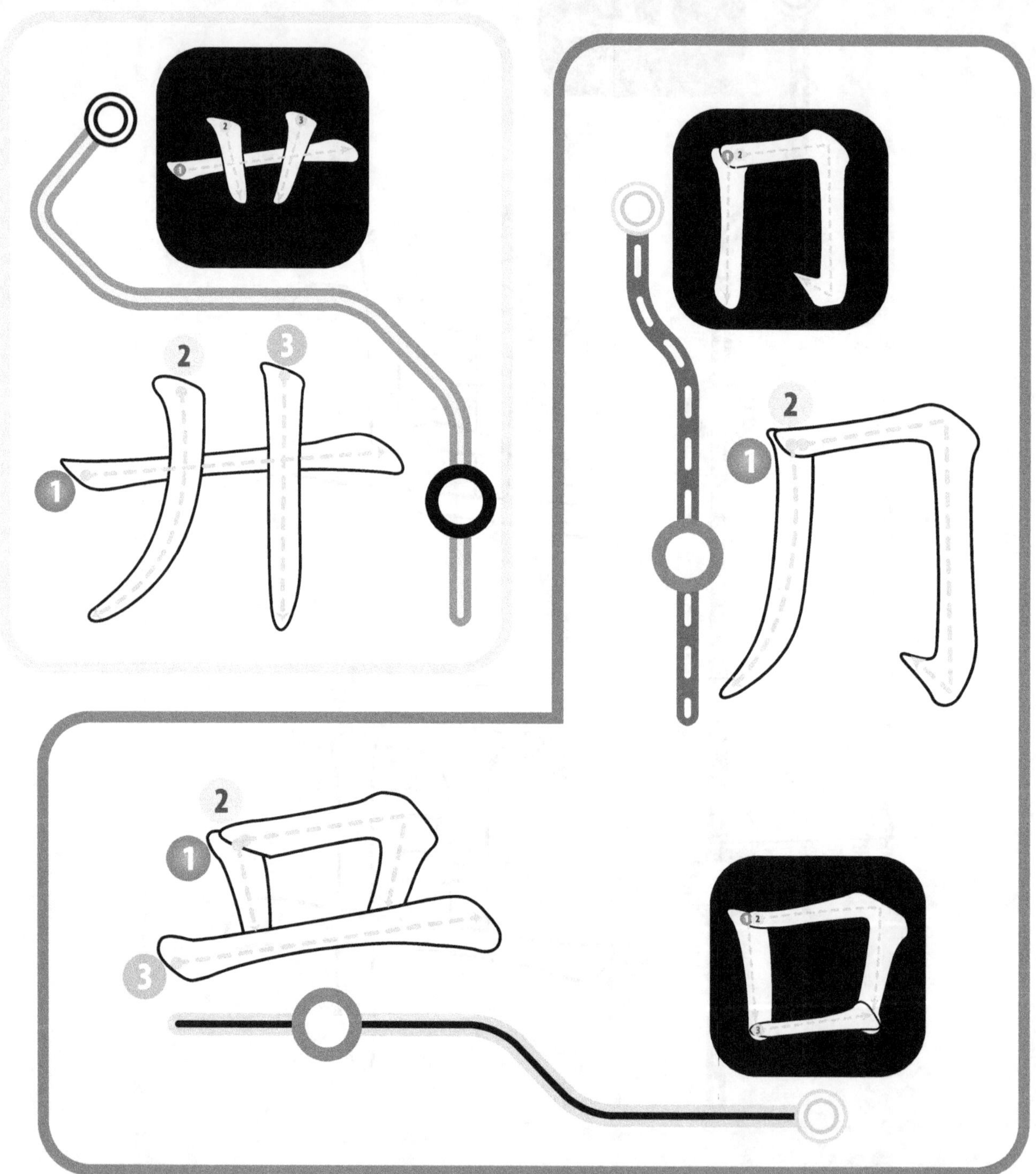

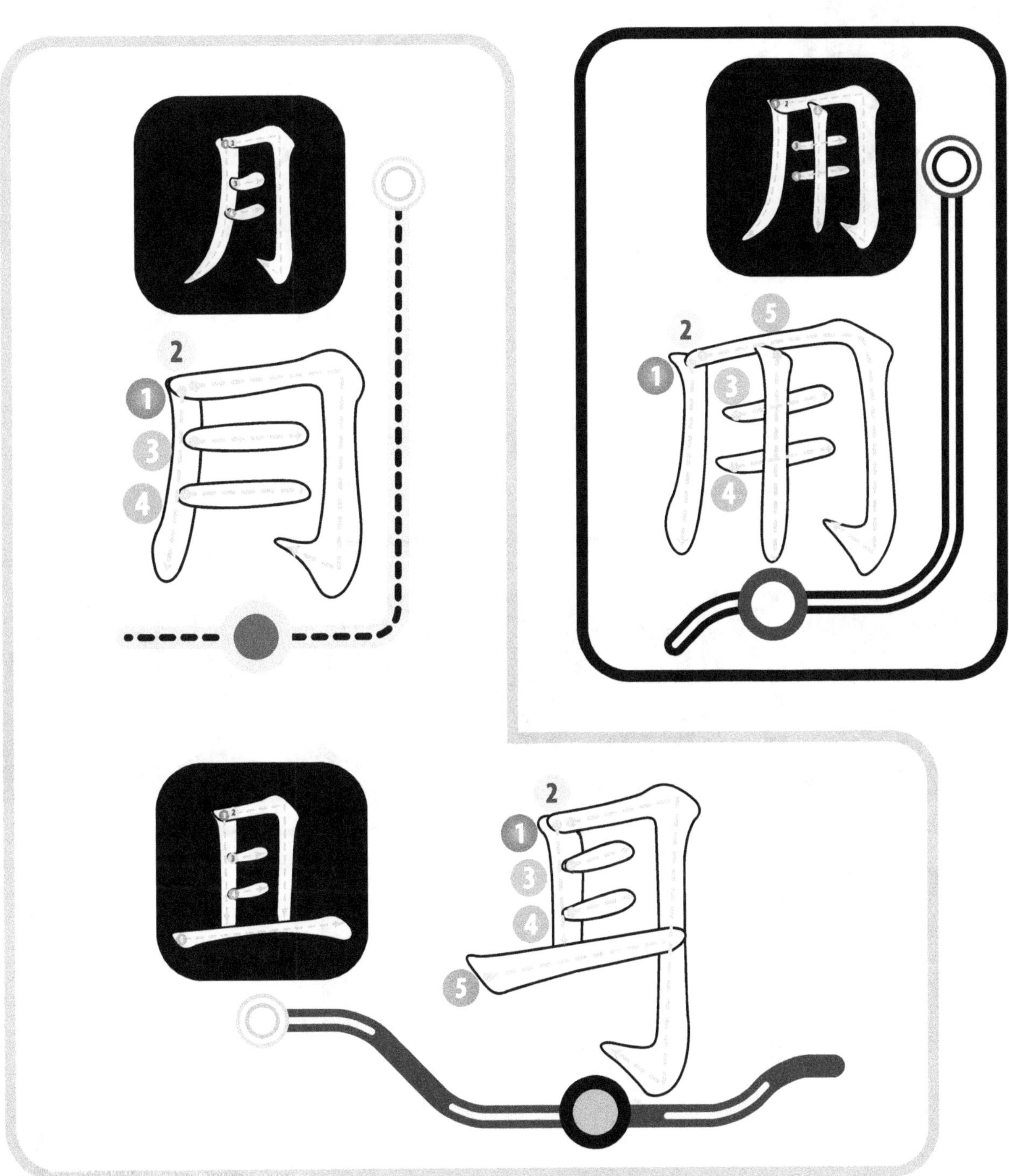

E1
Cross
Exception

Basic Alphabets

E2
Multiple Legs
Exception
Basic Alphabets

CHINESE ALPHABETS TRACING FOR TODDLERS

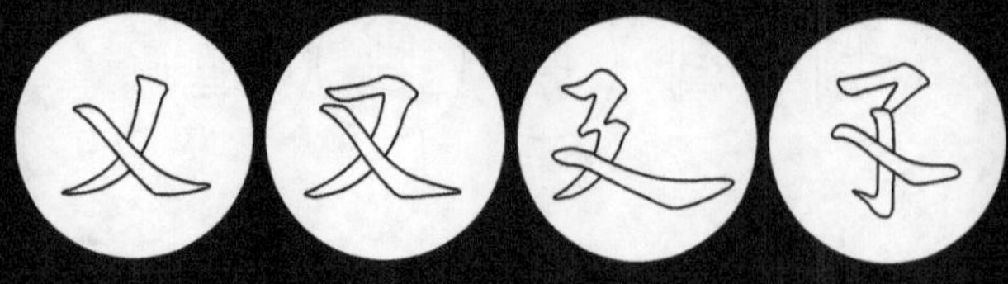

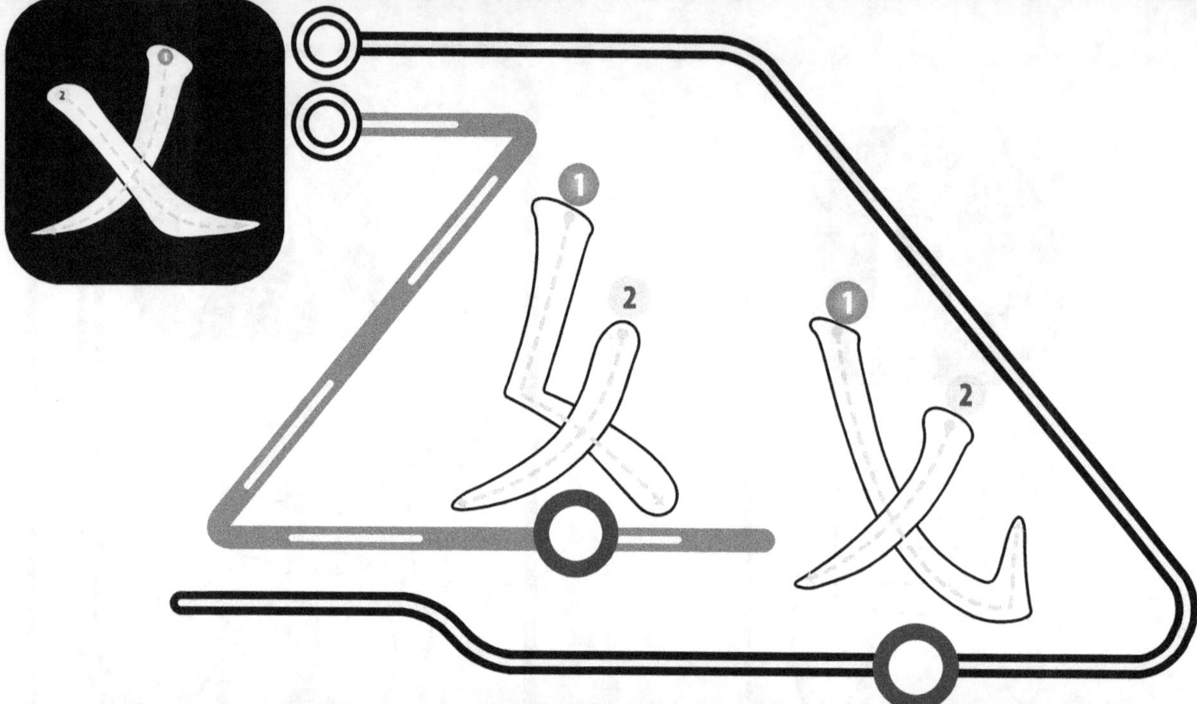

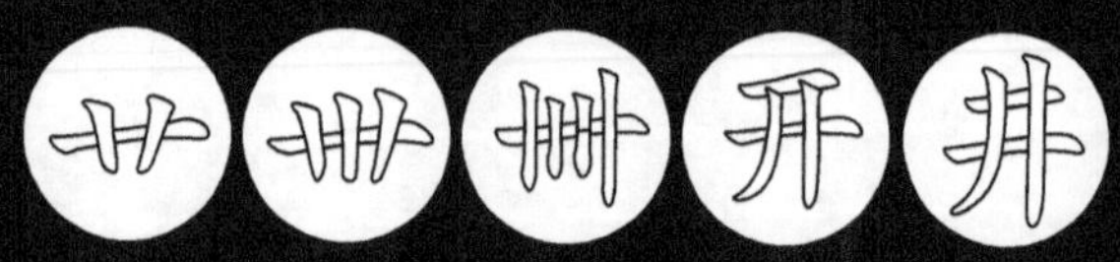

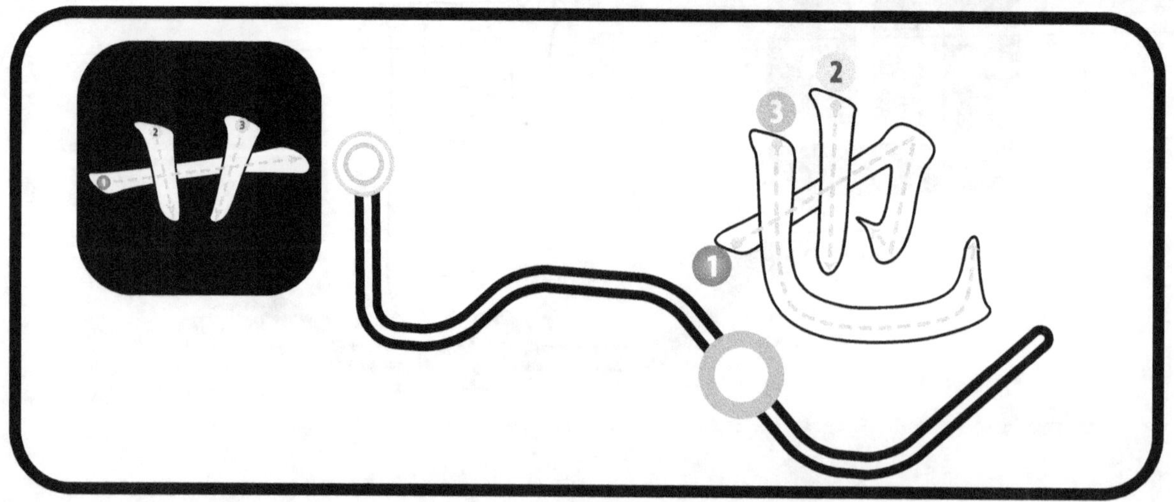

88